James Iverach

Theism in the Light of Present Science and Philosophy

James Iverach

Theism in the Light of Present Science and Philosophy

ISBN/EAN: 9783337080587

Printed in Europe, USA, Canada, Australia, Japan

Cover: Foto ©Lupo / pixelio.de

More available books at **www.hansebooks.com**

THEISM

IN THE LIGHT OF PRESENT SCIENCE AND PHILOSOPHY

BY

JAMES IVERACH, M.A., D.D.

AUTHOR OF "IS GOD KNOWABLE?" "EVOLUTION AND CHRISTIANITY," ETC.

PUBLISHED FOR

THE NEW YORK UNIVERSITY

BY

THE MACMILLAN COMPANY

1899

THE CHARLES F. DEEMS LECTURESHIP
OF PHILOSOPHY

THE University accepted, April 15, 1895, from the American Institute of Christian Philosophy an endowment of Fifteen Thousand Dollars for the support of a lectureship to be called the Charles F. Deems Lectureship of Philosophy, under the following rules : —

The University agrees to maintain said lectureship by securing for each year, or each alternate year, a Lecturer, eminent in Science and Philosophy, who shall treat in not less than six lectures some one of the most important questions of Science and Philosophy, with a special reference to its relation to the revealed truths of the Holy Scriptures and to the fundamental principles of Theistic Philosophy.

The Lecturer shall be chosen by the University's Committee upon the Charles F. Deems Lectureship, which shall consist of the Chancellor and two members of the Faculty of Arts and Science and two members of the University Council, to be named as the Council may direct.   The subject for each year's lectures shall be agreed upon between this Committee and the Lecturer.

The University shall provide, free of charge, a room for the lectures, and shall, at its own expense, make due public announcement of the time and place of each lecture. The University shall also publish, in book form, each series of lectures, and put the same on sale with one or more reputable book firms, provided this can be done without further expense than can be met by the accumulation of income over and above the expense of maintaining the annual or biennial series of lectures.

The University's Committee at present is constituted as follows: Chancellor MacCracken, Dean Baird, Dean Prince, Mr. William S. Opdyke, and Rev. Dr. George Alexander.

The inaugural course upon this foundation was given in April, 1899, by Professor James Iverach, D.D., of the Free Church College, Aberdeen, Scotland.

These lectures are now published by the University.

CONTENTS

CHAPTER IX

CHAPTER X

THEISM

IN THE LIGHT OF PRESENT SCIENCE AND PHILOSOPHY

THE SCIENTIFIC VIEW OF THE WORLD, AND ITS BEARING ON THEISM

My first duty in connection with this lectureship is to express my warmest thanks to the authorities of the New York University for the high honour they have conferred upon me in choosing me to be the first Deems lecturer. It is the greatest honour of my life, and it bears with it a corresponding responsibility. It came on me with surprise, and I accepted it with fear and anxiety; for I had some idea of the work done in America in theology and philosophy. I do not mention the achievements of America in other fields; I speak only of those with which I am familiar. It was surprising to me that I should be asked to speak to this University, and to this public, on topics with regard to which they had so many workers of renown on this side of the water. I had read many of the works of American writers on theology and philosophy; I had learned much from them; I had striven to follow the evolution of American thought and life, from the epoch-making work of Jonathan Edwards onward to the present time; and I had come to have a high appreciation of the value of that work. So numerous are the works of American writers on the subjects connected with the topic I have to discuss that I shall not mention any names. It you find in my lectures traces of the influence which your own writers have exerted on my mind, I hope you will not find fault with me on that account; I hope you will take it as a tribute to the value of American work.

The subject of my lecture is Theism, in the light of present science and philosophy. I shall endeavour to look at the world with the eyes of science, as science sets forth for us the story of the world in the ages of the past, and unfolds for us the magnificence of the world as it now is. I desire to learn from the masters of science what kind of world I live in, what has been its past history, and what is its probable outlook. Having learned from science all that I can grasp, I may have to ask questions which science cannot answer, ultimate questions which science leaves to philosophy and theology, and we shall ask what is the present attitude of philosophy toward these questions which science has left unsettled. It looks like a large order, and, on the face of it, it seems rather presumptuous for any man to profess to deal with so large a theme. It would be presumptuous were I to profess to teach all that science has to say on every topic, or even profess to have mastered all the sciences. I am not so presumptuous as to profess anything of the kind. A man may understand something of physics, although he has not read the "Principia" of Newton, and he may have a general knowledge of mathematics, though he is unfit to read all the works of Cayley or Sylvester. The scope and range of geological work he may understand, though he may not be familiar with all the details of the successive epochs of geological evolution. At all events, a man may study science for the purpose of seeing for himself that system of the universe which science may disclose to his mind, and may inquire what elements require to be added to the scientific view in order to obtain a rational view of the world as a whole. The presupposition of science is that the world has a meaning, is intelligible, and that the world is a whole, and forms a system. We presume that we are in a rational world, that things have a meaning, that they work together, and that the method of their working may be found and expressed. Acting on this presupposition men have gone to work, and in the several departments of science have formulated a number of rules or laws which have been verified as true, and when acted on have turned out to be adequate and accurate. Science, so far as it goes, is the record of man's understanding of the world in which he lives, and his mastery over it. I say so far as it goes; for great as have been its achievements, and vast as have been its conquests, it only stands on the threshold of the world it has to conquer. The world is one, and the sciences are many. The world moves together, and the sweep of its movement is always real, concrete, and complete. Our abstract sciences toil after it in vain. We break up the world into aspects, and we suffer for it; as each aspect tends to substitute itself in the place of the whole reality. The world thinks things together, we think them apart; and we are apt to put the aspect we see in the place of the whole.

It is our lot, as finite beings, to be able to attend to few things at a time. We have our ways of neglecting many aspects of reality, in order to attend only to that which attracts us, and to the understanding of which we bend all our strength. We have fallen on many methods by the use of which we seek to simplify the multiplicity of the problems set to us in life, and to make them such as we may grasp. We are baffled by the complex problems set to us by the simplest particle of matter. Even if we can picture to ourselves a particle of matter, it is impossible for us to grasp in one thought all that is involved in the notion. For there is in it, first, the notion of matter, which, simple as it appears to unreflective common sense, is yet one of the most complex notions which a long process of abstraction has bequeathed to us. Then it is by no means easy to grasp the notion of a particle, and the larger our knowledge is the more difficult is it to give a satisfactory account of a material particle. Suppose that we have come to some satisfactory definition of a particle of matter, such as we may find in our text-books of physics or chemistry, it is still too large for us to deal with it as a whole. In our statics we proceed to deal with it as it is at rest in its present position, whatever it may be, but in order to do so we must neglect all that is characteristic of it save only the one feature of it to which we attend. Then conceive it in motion, and we may deal with it under the title of the dynamics of a particle. Only those who have studied the mathematical complexities contained in a text-book with such a title can have any adequate conception of the intricate analysis and mathematical difficulty involved in a satisfactory treatment of the subject. In order to deal with it at all we have neglected all those aspects of the particle which do not lend themselves to our treatment. We simply treat it as a something which occupies space, and can be moved under certain forces from place to place. We do not think of it as having bulk, weight, resistance; nor do we think of it as being matter in a certain state. Temperature, chemical properties, electric condition, and a thousand other properties are non-existent for us, or, at all events, are neglected by us. In reality every particle of matter has physical, chemical, and other properties, and has them all at the same time. Every particle of matter has a certain weight, a certain chemical property, is at a certain temperature, and is in a certain electric state, but to grasp these all at once lies beyond our power. We need sometimes to remind ourselves of these most obvious truths. Amid the many and varied sciences that claim our attention, physics, — chemistry, biology, psychology, and so on, we are apt to think that the world of nature and of men is split up into so many compartments, which have little or no connection with one another. The separate sciences are apt to make us lose sight of the fact that we are dealing with one world. To limit our view at present to the inorganic world, let us think for a moment of the way in which we break up the unity of the world into aspects and fragments. I come to one of your great universities to study physics, and I put myself under the guidance of one of your great teachers. I am told that a certain amount of mathematical training is needed for the proper study of physics. I am told that all that has magnitude admits of measurement, and all that can be measured is subject to mathematics. I am taught mathematics, rising in time to its higher branches. The result is that I am led to look at the world as a great mechanism, working and being wrought in a way that can be calculated. It is a magnitude existing in space and time, and it works in a measurable fashion. That is the kind of notion given me by my study of mathematics.

Prepared thus, I go to a master in physics, and I find myself still in a world of mechanism, only now it is a world of a more intricate sort. There are bodies in it which I am told are real bodies. There are laws at work which I am told are real laws, and these I have to investigate and learn. I am taught that there are laws of motion, and I learn them as set forth by Newton, with whatever modifications of them have been made since his time. Properties of matter are set forth to me, and I am told of the various states which matter may assume; and I am told that whatever may be its state, it attracts all other matter in the universe inversely as the square of the distance. I learn something of the kinetic theory of gases, of the laws which govern matter in the gaseous, the liquid, and the solid state. But these states depend largely on temperature, and I must learn of heat and its laws, so the whole subject of thermo-dynamics opens up before me. This in turn is connected with electricity, and the subject of electricity next engages my attention. Suppose a man to be thus led around the whole round of physics as it is presented to him in any of our well-equipped universities, and to have acquired a well-grounded knowledge of the field of physics, what is his impression of it? It seems to me that the first thing he ought to do would be to touch mother earth once more. The unity of the physical world has been attenuated in his mind into a number of separate aspects. He has conceptions of a number of separate sciences, and of a world which so far corresponds to each abstract science, but not of a world which corresponds to the unity which underlies them all. Light, heat, electricity, gravitation, properties of matter, all the separate sciences which make up the whole conception of physics, lie as separate sciences in the mind, and the need of a concrete universal is great. Even the great doctrine of the conservation of energy is insufficient to bring our physicist back to concrete reality, for it, too, is an abstraction.

We are so proud, too, of our abstractions, and of those general laws which we have been able to express. We grow eloquent about the law of gravitation, of the conservation of energy, and other great generalizations which mark the greatness of the human mind. Men talk grandly of the persistence of force, and think they can explain the universe in terms of matter and motion, and their distribution and redistribution. I do not find fault; but I seek to remember that the explanations which I read are not in terms of the reality of the world, but in terms of the abstractions which have been made by finite intelligence, and that they may have only a finite reference. The process of abstraction and generalization, by means of which we seek to pass from the particular to the universal, lead us farther and farther from reality. Certain aspects are isolated. We take those qualities in which particular things resemble each other, and we neglect the differences, and we invent general names for those qualities they have in common. When the process is so far complete, we are apt to substitute the qualities we have abstracted for the complex reality of which they are only aspects. It helps us to call green, violet, red, by the general name of colour, it helps our thinking to have a general name for plants, animals, men, and so on, if we remember that the unity thus manufactured is only formal, made by us for our convenience, and does not represent a real unity. It is no real bond of union that we reach by a process of generalization. In fact, the more we generalize, the farther do we remove ourselves from reality; and the objective truth of things cannot be reached by that process.

Our books on logical and scientific method teach with sufficient fulness and clearness the process by which we rise to the recognition of wider and wider laws. Here they leave nothing to be desired. Our university lectures also teach the theory of the process of generalization adequately and fully. I do not find in our books descriptive of scientific and logical method what I find in the practical teaching of science. There I am taught not only to rise to higher and higher generalizations, I am taught to recognize that synthesis of particulars which constitute the thinghood of the thing. This reverse process is in fact always going on. The process of science depends not only on the recognition of wider generalizations, but also on the discovery of those unities which have features peculiar to themselves. It was a great discovery to find out the mechanical equivalent of heat, and to be able to say that heat is a mode of motion; it was also a discovery quite as great to find out Argon, with its unique characteristics. General laws are, after all, not the greatest part of human knowledge, nor the most important. While we speak about them and use them, we always do so with a kind of unconscious caution, and with the reserve that they must conform to the objective reality. Our practical teachers, who have always before them the tremendous criticism which nature passes on our abstractions, insist that their students shall have, not only a knowledge of abstract mathematics and physics, but they also insist that students shall make themselves acquainted with the qualities and characteristics of those materials with which they will have to deal in the active business of their profession. Thus the concrete particularity of each kind of thing is of the utmost importance; and the method of ascertaining these is not recognized in our text-books.

Still, it may be admitted that the attainment of universality is eminently desirable. To be able to make universal judgments is indeed indispensable. How shall they be made? Generalization, or the method which arrives at a kind of universality by leaving out differences, does not seem a hopeful method. True, we may thus arrive at a certain kind of universality, but when we have done so, it is a kind which has no objective reference, and is not true save of our subjective notions. That there are a unity and universality in things is a conviction as deep as any to be found in the human mind; but how shall we attain to that unity? May we hope to find a universality which will not express merely the invention of the observing and classifying mind, but a unity and universality immanent in the things themselves, and expressive of their very nature? May we hope to find a method which shall take up particular things in all their particularity, and yet see them, not in isolation, but in their relation to the system of which they form a part? It were a consummation devoutly to be wished. Certainly there is such a system, and the intelligible universe is such a system. There, in concrete reality, are the things, beings, persons, actually subsisting in one space and in one time, each in its concrete reality, with all its peculiarities and characteristics; and without suppression of difference they take their place and perform their functions in the ongoing of the universe. We shall never reach any nearer to an apprehension of the real universe by running upward to the highest abstraction we can express, — call it substance, being, or force, or by any other name, — and then reverse the process and descend downward, adding difference to difference as we need them, till we arrive at the concrete world. We are in an unreal world all the time, and our abstractions simply delude us. Worlds are not made in that way, nor can they by that way be understood.

In our descriptions and definitions we take what we conceive to be essential, positive, and sufficient, and we are ready to forget those qualities which we have left out of account. By simply taking those properties which we have abstracted from the concrete reality, we have not caused the other relations to disappear. They remain as a disturbing element, to remind us again of their neglected existence. Those which we have regarded as essential properties, fixed in a definition, and marked by a common name, are real; but the neglected are also real. Matter may be described as a set of individual units, or as a set of things bound together in chemical relations, but neither conception expresses all that we mean by matter. Each expresses one aspect of real existence, and we may use it without error, so long as we remember that it represents only an aspect, and that aspect the one we are most interested in for the time.

We do injustice to the actual procedure of scientific men when we formulate it as we have done in our text-books of logic. Conceptions, general names, notions, are set forth as if they are the results of a process of abstraction, in which specific differences are neglected and left out of account. The real process of science, as exemplified by the practice of scientific men, is something very different. It is the attempt to recognize in things the concrete relations to each other which they involve. I do not think I can describe it better than by a description of the process of an actual discovery. Professor Ramsay, in the conclusion of an article on "The Kinetic Theory of Gases," in the *Contemporary Review*, says: "We have seen that the discovery by Lord Rayleigh of a discrepancy in the density of atmospheric nitrogen has resulted in the discovery of a new constituent of air, argon; its discovery has led to that of a constituent of the solar atmosphere, helium; speculations on the ultimate nature and motion of the particles of which it is believed that gases consist has provoked the consideration of the conditions necessary in order that planets and satellites may retain an atmosphere, and of the nature of that atmosphere; the necessary existence of an undiscovered element was foreseen, owing to the usual regularity in the distribution of the atomic weights of elements not being attained in the case of helium and argon, and the source of neon was therefore indicated. This source, atmospheric air, was investigated, and the missing element was discovered. A new fact has been added to science, and one not disconnected from others, but one resulting from the convergence of many speculations, observations, and theories, brought to bear on one another." (*Contemporary Review*, November, 1898, p. 691.)

Here we have a telling illustration of the difference between the universal as a law of nature and the universal which is merely an abstract conception.

In the wonderful story of scientific success recorded by Professor Ramsay, we never touch the region of mere abstract conceptions. There is first the recognition of the difference of density between nitrogen from one source and another, and there is the intelligent search for the cause of this difference. The result is the discovery of an element having properties distinct from all other elements. Here is the search for a concrete thing successfully conducted, and there is no parade of abstract formulæ employed in the search. At the basis there is a magnificent conception; but it is one not reached by a process of mere generalization arrived at by leaving out specific differences. It is reached by recognizing the specific differences of all the elements known, their mutual relations, and the laws of their distribution, and thus a new element is added to the family of chemical elements. It is to be observed, also, that a regard to the law of periodicity of the weights of the elements led on to the further discovery of neon. The beauty of the real process of discovery, whether it be the discovery of a new element, or of a wide law like that known as the "periodic arrangement of elements," is that it is no abstract conception that is reached, but a conception which strives to set forth clearly, fully, adequately, the concrete relations of the objects in view. A conception which correctly formulates the actual relations of things has thus real objective value. Taken by itself it is a mere abstraction, and is only a symbol, which may mislead the mind by a false appearance of reality.

The difference here emphasized between a scientific conception and a mere abstract conception is dwelt upon because it will greatly help us in the course of our discussion. To take an illustration which may anticipate what will be more fully discussed later on, but is used here to show why we have insisted on the distinction. Spinoza says, " Omnis determinatio est negatio "; and this has been made the basis of much argumentation of the negative sort. It has been applied to the theistic argument; it has been used to show that the absolute and infinite are only negative notions. If we are perched on the ladder of generalization as it is described in a book of pure logic, it is true that every definition limits. We mark this object out from others by its positive qualities and its specific difference. But when we pass on to the consideration of a concrete being in all its manifoldness of concrete qualities, we simply reverse the maxim of Spinoza, and say, " Omnis determinatio est affirmatio." We go on to add quality to quality until we have summed up the whole of the qualities of this being in its concrete unity and reality. The larger the number of qualities, and the higher the rank of qualities sphered in any one being, the greater we reckon that being to be. Every attribute we see in that being, and express in our notion of it, is not a negation of any quality which it may be supposed to possess, but an affirmation of the truth that the being has this particular excellence in addition to all the others we have spoken of, and possesses them in the harmony of one existence. Conceptions which have real worth, that is, those conceptions which express the immanent nature and relations of the concrete world, are set free from the merely negative limitation set by the maxim of Spinoza, and rejoice in the freedom of doing real positive work, and of building up a world of real knowledge which will approximate closer and closer to the world of real existence. But this is the real method and work of science when we regard it in the practice of the masters of science, who have widened the boundaries of knowledge. No doubt, Spinoza tells us ("Ethics," Book I., Prop. IX.), that "the more reality or being a thing has, the greater the number of its attributes," but that is only to say that Spinoza sometimes forgot his axiom, "Omnis determinatio est negatio," for by this axiom we can reach nothing save the most general and empty abstraction, being without attributes, a mere indeterminate something. It was not the purpose of Spinoza to start from being in general, or to reach that conception as the outcome of his reasoning. He desired to attain to the knowledge of the absolute totality of things, conceived as a unity in which all particular existences might find a place and serve as elements in an intelligible whole. He has a real apprehension of the unreal and imaginary character of mere conceptions, and he warns his readers against them. Straightway he himself falls under their yoke, and actually proceeds according to the method of abstraction. Being with no attributes at all gives place to the most determinate being conceivable, namely, being constituted by an infinite number of attributes. What he did accomplish was to dissolve all into the ultimate abstraction of being from which there was no way of return to an actual world; what he meant to do was to relate all the parts to that absolute being which he conceived to be the presupposition of thought and being, and the unity of all existence. His is a conspicuous instance of the fate which befalls great thinkers and great systems, when they depart from a method which alone can conserve the manifold relations of reality with a regard to the necessity of thinking them as related parts of a system.

Being attenuated till it is altogether without attributes, substance, without any determination or characterization, force, or the persistence of force, gives no intelligible starting-point for the knowledge of reality. These are merely abstractions, easy to reach, and worthless when we have reached them. Leaving them on one side and following in the steps of the masters of science who have striven to see the world in its actual movement, let us see what kind of world is revealed to us through their guidance.

c

It is an intelligible world, a world existing in one space and in one time, a world which moves under law.   No doubt our masters present that world to us under aspects, and each presents it under that aspect in which he is most interested, and with which he is most familiar.   It takes many sciences to bring us near to the real world, but by bringing the sciences together we may come to some apprehension of the magnificence of the world.   At least we may have some notion of the complexity and simplicity of the world, and that it looks like a work worthy of an infinite intelligence.   It is a greater world than our fathers dreamt of, it has lengthened in time, broadened in space, and has a wider sweep of order and a vaster rhythm than men thought of till recent thoughts were apprehended by the human mind. The story of the making of the worlds is written on the wastes of space, and carried on the waves of light to the remotest stars.   When we go out on a clear starlight night and look up to the Milky Way, or gaze on the bands of Orion, at first we think that we are reading a contemporary story.   We are soon told, and it is difficult to realize it, that we are reading pages of the history of the universe, some written a thousand years ago and some yesterday.   I am not to trouble with figures, which might be easily given, but it may be said that the light which falls on our eyes tells us of the state of the star from which it comes as that star was when the light started on its tremulous way. It tells us of the state of that star when Marathon was fought, so long it has taken to reach us across the depths of space. Inconceivable magnitudes, distances unimaginable, yet across them light can travel, and the ether, the undulations of which are light, stretches all the way. Had we eyes to read the story of what we see on any evening on which we look up to the starry heavens, what a story it would be. The drama of the separate worlds which make up the universe of matter might be read there. There are worlds in the making, some of them only in their infancy, not yet arrived at definite form. There are masses of glowing gas, the raw material of ordered worlds, masses gathered into something like form, worlds in the full maturity of worldhood, and worlds that seemingly have had their day, and have passed into the ways of decay.

Everywhere, too, as these worlds and systems exist in one space and one time, so they seem to be built up of the same kind of stuff, and to be ruled by the same laws that obtain on this earth. The light that reaches us from the most distant star may be broken up and dispersed on its arrival here, and on being wisely asked will tell us what were the conditions of its source, and what were the elements of matter that sent it forth. The main thing for me is that there is a story to tell, and a story which we have so far read, so far at least as to give us reason to believe that it is an intelligible story. Written in the light that speeds across space, told by the light itself as it reaches us, do you not think that if our intelligence can read it, some intelligence akin to ours instructed the light to record it? At all events we may rest in the belief that we are in one universe with the most distant body in space, that light there and here is constituted the same way, and that there is one medium which makes the transmission of light possible. Nor is this the only universal statement we can make about the universe. The stuff which makes up our world is the same stuff made up in the same kinds as we know on the earth and in the solar system. Hydrogen is hydrogen, vibrating in the same time, emitting or absorbing the same light as it does here. The same attractions and repulsions characterize the matter of the stars, and the particles of matter attract each other directly as the masses and inversely as the square of the distance. This seems true of all material worlds, that they are made of the same stuff, and are ruled by the same laws. Along with the sameness which unites them, there seems to be endless variety in the systems which occur in the sidereal heavens. Systems of binary stars revolving round a common centre of gravity, systems like our solar system only more complex, and systems so varied and complex that they pass our understanding. Nay, science is dreaming of an earlier evolution, lying beyond the stage of atoms and molecules, as these are known to us. It dreams of a pre-atomic state of matter, in which the so-called atoms of the chemist represent not the origin of things, but only early stages of the evolutionary process. Science deems that at present in the atmospheres of the suns and stars there are forces at work which prevent the formation of atoms and molecules, such as are aggregated at the temperature of the earth. However that may be, and we may wish our scientific friends success in every attempt to widen the bounds of human knowledge, certain it is that in the systems that make up the material universe we know of matter in all the stages of evolution. There are stars which are growing hotter, stars at their maximum of heat, stars and systems that are growing cooler. Worlds in the making, worlds made, and worlds passing into decay; we are bewildered with the magnificence of the world disclosed to us by science. It is an ordered world which we are called on to contemplate. If there is a pre-atomic state of matter, it exists under other conditions than those which obtain on the earth, and our means of dissociation are too limited to enable us to reproduce that condition of matter. For us, atoms are ultimate and cannot be brought to a finer shape. This, also, has a bearing on the intelligibility of the world which is a postulate of theism. The original stuff is made with a bias, and has an invincible tendency to aggregate itself into certain irreversible patterns. Chemical elements are formed which maintain their identity and continuity in all circumstances, and no amount of work which we can bring to bear on them can break them up into simpler forms. One stuff which at certain temperatures passes into irreversible forms; forms which abide amid all changes as the elementary atoms out of which ordered systems are built up; this simply gives us a wider, grander purpose than we were wont to think of. In that primitive state of matter there is an inherent tendency to aggregate itself into certain abiding forms, and these forms have certain properties and relations which enable them to build up a stable system, and on that stable system there have been built other systems, such as life, intelligence, a mind capable of reading the whole story. Such is the kind of universe we live in.

When we pass from astronomical physics to the world which chemistry discloses to our view we come to a story equally wonderful, and equally intelligible. These atoms which to us are ultimate have properties which can be understood. They are of various kinds, each perfect in its kind, and are related to each other in such a way as to form a system. To describe them would simply be to transcribe what is within the reach of every one. Their weights, their combining properties, their preference for one combination rather than another, their periodicity, which is so remarkable that elements were predicted, their properties described before they were discovered, reveal to us an ordered world which may well arouse our admiration, and reward our investigation. Taking for granted the facts disclosed to us by chemistry and the theoretic conclusions established by chemists, we observe that we have made an advance and have become acquainted with a new set of properties and laws. Gravitation is still with us, and matter still attracts matter according to a certain law, temperature abides, force, as we knew it in physics, remains, but we become acquainted with other forces and other laws than those we knew in physics. Two elementary bodies combine together on certain conditions, and stick together until work is done on them to make them part. Each atom of matter has its own way of action, and insists on combining with others, only on its own conditions. Many other things might be said had we time. These are said, however, for the purpose of showing that chemistry is compelled to make its own assumptions, and it certainly has the right to do so. You may say that here we are still in the domain of mechanism, and are working under the dominion of mechanical law. I am not disposed to quarrel about terms, but if you insist on calling this mechanical, you must recognize a difference in the physical and chemical mechanical assumptions. In physics you deal only with the relations which can be subsumed under gravitation, heat, and so on; in chemistry you deal with attractions and repulsions of another order. Oxygen and hydrogen do not obey the law of inverse squares, nor can you calculate the law of repulsion of atoms in an explosive mixture. Or if you can make the calculation, you must use a calculus other than that which you use in mere physics. I make this observation for the purpose of showing that each science has its own method, makes its own assumptions, and deals with its own subject in its own way. I shall have occasion to say this frequently as we pass on, and I make it broadly now. A physical problem is one thing, a chemical problem is another; physical dynamics is approached in one way, a problem in chemical dynamics is solved only by a chemical method. These observations are necessary in view of the vast generalizations in some of the great systems in vogue at the present hour, in which it is assumed that the method and the assumptions of physics are sufficient for the explanation of the universe. It is assumed that mechanical law is sufficient for the explanation of all phenomena. On the contrary, we find that this is insufficient, even for the explanation of the simplest problem in chemistry. For physics deals only with ponderable matter, while chemistry deals with its own conception of energies arising from intrinsic differences of matter, and consequently it penetrates into a region inaccessible to physics. It may be possible to arrive at a dynamic of the energy set up by the interaction of chemical elements, but this will be a mechanism of a finer order. The contention is that the method of the simpler, more abstract, science is inadequate to deal with problems of another order. No doubt physics is helpful to chemistry, as both are helpful in biology, and all three are helpful in psychology, but the helpfulness would cease, or become hurtfulness, if they attempted to rule out all they could not grasp. As we shall see, this is constantly being done, to the injury of clear thinking; and fruitful progress in our attempt to understand the world in its concrete reality is hindered by over-generalization, and by the extension of a method beyond its limits.

When we unite the results of physics and chemistry, we reach a fuller view of reality than when we look at the world with the eyes of each separately. We recognize that matter is one, and that matter is made up of parts; that there is an energy of mass and position, and also an energy arising out of the relations of different kinds of matter each to each. The uniformity of mechanical law which has regard only to impressed force is supplemented by the law of attraction known as chemical affinity, and the compounds arising out of chemical combination. Masses count, but atoms count also; and there is the unity of many elements in one system.

Ere we leave the vision of the world disclosed to us by physics and chemistry, let us take a glance at another aspect of their work. These sciences deal not only with those aspects of reality which have already been mentioned, they strive to deal with the unseen agent or medium which has been postulated to account for the phenomena of light, and other related phenomena. Assumed to account for the phenomena of light, it has been found necessary for the understanding of other phenomena. The characteristics of the ether are thus set forth by Clerk Maxwell: "It appears, therefore, that certain phenomena in electricity and magnetism lead to the same conclusion as those of optics; namely, that there is an ætherial medium pervading all bodies, and modified only in degree by their presence; that the parts of this medium are capable of being set in motion by electric currents and magnets; that this motion is communicated from one part of the medium to another by forces arising from the connection of these parts; that under the action of these forces there is a certain yielding depending on the elasticity of these connections; and that, therefore, energy in two different forms may exist in the medium, the one form being the actual energy of motion of its parts, the other being the potential energy stored up in the connections in virtue of their elasticity. Thus, then, we are led to the conception of a complicated mechanism capable of a vast variety of motion, but at the same time so connected that the motion of one part depends, according to definite relations, on the motion of other parts, these motions being communicated by forces arising from the relative displacement of the connected parts, in virtue of their elasticity. Such a mechanism must be subject to the general laws of dynamics, and we ought to be able to work out all the consequences of its motion, provided we know the form of the relation between the motions of the parts." (Quoted in Glazebrook's "James Clerk Maxwell and Modern Physics," p. 179.)

Maxwell was able to deduce the mechanical and electric actions which take place, and these have been verified by subsequent experiment. Wireless telegraphy and other wonderful phenomena illustrate the insight of Maxwell, and bear witness to the existence of the mechanism of the ether, the stresses of which seem equally related to the phenomena and electricity and light, if these are not at bottom one and the same, as they are certainly most intimately related. I mention these things without dwelling on them, as I desire to call attention to the boldness of the conception and the magnificence of the results worked out by means of it. To suppose a medium filling all space, pervading all forms of matter in every state of matter, stresses in which can be propagated with the speed of light across the spaces of the universe, which could be a means of communication between the worlds which make up the universe, and to be able to say what must be the properties, or, at least, what some of its properties must be, was certainly a bold conception, and a great achievement of the

human mind. If to discover such a medium and
to investigate its properties is a great triumph of
intelligence, what must the reality be? Suppose
the ether to exist in the form and with the qualities and functions described by Clerk Maxwell, and
with other properties and functions unrecognized as
yet, are we simply to recognize the fact, accept it
as ultimate, and pass on? Is that all? Are we to
recognize the functions of the ether, to see clearly
enough that the existence of some such medium
and of such work as is done by means of it is the
condition of light and heat in a world otherwise
dark, cold, and lifeless, and are we not to be allowed
to think of a purpose and meaning in connection
with its function and work? It took intelligence of
a high order to discover the existence and meaning of the ether: has the existence of it no relation to intelligence? Are we simply to accept it
as a fact and think no more about it? That is the
attitude which many assume, while some go further
and say to us with more or less authority, that
order, law, and mechanism are ultimate, and when
we find these we can dispense with intelligence.
That raises the question of the relation of order
and intelligence, and as to whether the human
mind can ever rest in any explanation of the order
of the world which leaves it unrelated to intelligence. Leaving aside all questions as to the seat
of the intelligence, whether immanent or tran-

scendent, within or without the world, surely on the general question there can be no manner of hesitation as to the answer of a rational being, conscious that he is in a rational universe. We know that the world, as it appears to science, has a most definite relation to intelligence. Science is the work of mind, of the intelligence of a succession of thinkers, who received the work from them who went before and handed it down to those who bore the torch onward to ever larger results. If we bow in reverence before those who made science, and gratefully recognize the worth and greatness of their intelligence, what is to be our attitude in presence of the great reality of the universe, so much greater than the mind of the wisest, ablest, and greatest of men can conceive? Is there not in the phenomena of the universe, roughly outlined, traces of an intelligence akin to the intelligence of Newton and Maxwell? Of the character of that intelligent power manifest in the universe, disclosed to us by physics and chemistry, we are able to say nothing further at present, save that the intelligence is of an order equal to the production of the phenomena. Look at it from the mechanical point of view, consider the phenomena of the ether, its relations to ponderable matter, and the functions it performs in the universe ; and can we not say that as it has a meaning, so it must have a purpose? Think of the vastness of the

movement of the universe, of its interrelations, of
its sweep through time, everchanging but changing in a way that can be understood, working out
coördinated harmonics of the most magnificent
kind, some of which we can read, and shall we
not say that the grandest thing we know is present here?

At all events, whether our men of science allow
us to say that mind is here or whether they do not
allow us, we may feel grateful to them for the conception they have enabled us to form of the magnificence of the universe. They have enabled us to
look out at the wonder of the universe as it seems
to exist now; they have taught us to look back on
an illimitable past, and to see the evolving worlds
on their way to something, and they show us that
everywhere there are method, order, law. If they
insist that we shall simply rest content in the grandeur they enable us to see, and constrain us to
regard it as an ultimate fact, well, we must part
company with them at this point, and respectfully
say that we must take up our burden without them,
and seek to interpret the facts for ourselves. A
system that at this end needs an intelligence to
understand it must have something to do with intelligence at the other end. Such a one-sided reference as is presented to us by them is, to speak with
all respect, scarcely intelligible. At present we are
content to rest our case on the fact of order, and to

say that order implies intelligence. The greatness of the order, the vastness of the rhythm of the universe, may increase our wonder and deepen our apprehension of the greatness of the intelligence which caused and made the order, but it does not increase the strength of the argument.

We then go on, whether science accompanies us or no. We cannot rest in the mere discovery of the order, law, method of procedure, of the universe. This, for us, can never be ultimate. We know of one kind of cause which can account for an order that can be understood, and we know of only one. We know intelligence as it has produced the works of artists, poets, philosophers, men of science, and we do not know enough to put any limit on the extent and kind of work which intelligence may produce. True, the intelligence which we know is not quite of the creative kind, it works within the limits of human experience, and in most cases it is striving to read a meaning already given in the facts of nature. But the intelligence that we know—limited, conditioned, receptive though it be—is yet sufficient to give us the idea of an intelligence which has no limits, to which we can set no bounds, which can set the bounds to the material on which it acts and prescribe its nature, and the method of its working.

I have made no remark about the fact that there is power at work in the universe, because that fact is not disputed.　Nor is it questioned that the power at work in the universe is a regulated power that works according to a plan, and produces intelligible results.　Even Mr. Herbert Spencer asserts as much as this.　He can speak of "an infinite and eternal energy from which all things proceed."　He will not, indeed, allow us to say anything regarding it save that it is.　It is, he says, absolutely unknowable, and yet he can speak of it as energy, as infinite and as eternal.　It works in the universe, and the method of its working Mr. Spencer claims to have traced and described in the synthetic philosophy, and yet he says that it is unknowable.　If it has manifested itself, it surely can be known, at least as far as it has manifested itself.　But we do not deal with Mr. Spencer's argument at present.　I cite his view, that there is power in the universe. I call it an intelligible power because it works by methods which I can partially understand, to results which are orderly and intelligible.　As has been often observed, I have no other ground than this for the inference that the moving bodies I see in the street are men and women with an intelligence like my own.　The grounds of inference are the same, and the inference from intelligible results to an intelligence are precisely the same.

True, the intelligence which informs the universe is as much greater than mine as the universe is greater than my thought of it.　What then?　The

power at work in the universe is greater than any
which I can exert, but that has not hindered men
from speaking of an infinite and eternal energy.
It is as legitimate to speak of an eternal intelligence
as to speak of an eternal energy.

So far then we have come as to have good grounds
for saying that the power at work in the world is
an intelligent power; we proceed to ask whether we
can fairly say anything more about that power.

D

II

THE INORGANIC WORLD A PREPARATION FOR LIFE: THE PHYSICAL CHARACTERISTICS OF LIFE

TAKING the universe as a whole, as disclosed to us by science, we have learned that it can be understood. We infer, also, that it has a meaning wider far than the meaning we have been able to grasp. Our reading of it is somewhat vague and indefinite, and we see that it comes far short of the fulness of meaning in the concrete reality. So far we have seen only aspects of the reality, but these aspects are set in relation to intelligence. Narrowing our sphere of operations, and coming to those modes of existence nearer to us than the fixed stars, limiting our view to the system of which our own planet forms an integral part, let us ask here, too, the guidance of science. I again take from science simply what I need. Following the lead of science I read a wondrous story. I am led back into a past that begins long ago. The story of our system that is told began some fifty million years ago. That beginning is not absolute, it is only the stage at which science takes up the story of the solar system. It does not pretend to speak of the stages of the history of the solar system, before the material of it lay as an attenuated cloud of nebulous matter stretching from the centre, out on all sides to the utmost bounds of the orbit of the most distant planet. That mass of nebulous matter being given, subject to the ordinary attractions and repulsions, and other properties characteristic of matter, it has been thought that the evolution of the solar system may be explained. Difficulties of various kinds may be raised, but I do not raise them now. For whatever may be made of them, and however perplexing they may be, there is no doubt that some form of the nebular theory is true. At all events we may have a clear vision of our planet existing as a molten globe, moving in an orbit not widely different from the orbit traced out by it at present, in its annual circuit around the sun. The double revolution round its own axis and round the sun are there, and the consequences of these movements can be traced on the shape and form of the earth. The form of the earth is precisely that which a molten body, moving under such conditions, would assume.

Starting afresh from that position, and tracing out the results of it, science reads for us the life history of the earth so far as it can. A body slowly cooling in the same way as bodies do cool, with the regulated changes of form, which ensue on the process of cooling, with the chemical changes of material form, which arise when a lowered temperature allows chemical affinity to have freedom of action. There comes a time when the earth obtains a solid crust. A series of changes worked out under law leads on to an earth with a diversified surface. Into the details of geology it is not necessary to enter. They are familiar and easily accessible. The stately procession of orderly facts may be read in any text-book of value. As we read we see that we are led on from the more simple to the more complex, from a state of matter comparatively simple to a state of the utmost complexity, from a stuff comparatively homogeneous to one highly heterogeneous; and we are constrained to think not of a unity made up of one property, but of a unity constituted out of many elements held together in virtue of their relations each to each and each to the whole. The differentiations become more numerous and more decisive, while the unity becomes more distinct.

The story of the evolution of the inorganic world is long, and full of interest, and, whether they mean to do so or not, our scientific guides have told it — have, in fact, been constrained to tell it — as a preparation for the introduction of life. I do not think they meant to tell the story so, but they have told it, and have shown us a world actually being prepared for the introduction of life. What a series of converging conditions was needed in order to make life possible, as life exists on the earth. Apart from the question of whether this convergence of conditions was intended or no, we lay stress on the fact that the convergence is there, and the result is the same as if they were meant. To enumerate some of these conditions: The distance of the earth from the sun; the revolution of the earth round its own axis, which makes the succession of day and night possible; the circuit of the earth round the sun, which gives the succession of seedtime and harvest, summer and winter; the distribution of the surface of the earth into land and water, elevations and depressions; the great fact that the earth was enabled somehow to keep those chemical elements which are indispensable to life, so that even the most volatile of them should not escape into the wastes of space; the capacity of these elements to be worked up to higher levels and to more complex forms under the touch of life; the relations of the atmosphere and the qualities of it, and the seemingly exact calculation of the range of temperature within which life would be possible, — these are some of the conditions which have converged in order to make life possible on the earth.

These are not, however, all the conditions which might be set forth in this connection, but they are sufficient for our purpose. Observe the story is told by science and told in its own way. It is dealing, according to its wont, with a system of efficient causes.

It has not gone beyond its own sphere, and has made no assumptions beyond what it can verify. It has called on no forces save those which are at work now. It told us of the molten earth, of its gradual cooling, of its consolidation, of the slow differentiation into air, water, land; it told of igneous rocks, of their denudation, of the wearing down of rocks and the building of rocks, and of many other processes, all told in the way of science; and then it told us of the introduction of life, and showed to us the first trace of life at a certain geological epoch. We find on reading the story that it has been telling us a story of preparations for the introduction of life. We are inclined to say there is a Divinity that shapes our ends, rough-hew them as we will.

I do not expect them to draw the inference that I draw. Indeed, many of the men of science expressly repudiate such an inference, and get quite angry and say hard things of the capacity of those who venture to draw such an inference. Well, if I were to tell the story of the introduction of life from the point of view of purpose, I would tell it in precisely the same way and in the same terms as it has been told by science. Long preparations stretching to the bounds of conceivable time, reaching to the farthest world, ether with its undulations, matter in all its qualities, all set in certain relations, and made to take a certain course through millions of years, and life becomes possible, and life is. I call it a purposive line of action, and who has the right to gainsay me? I have followed the leading of science, and as I followed I saw that it used its own method, and no other. The conception of causality, nay, the conception of mechanical causation, was the main conception through which science looked at the changes of the history of the world, and we find that even that conception led us on to this result, that mechanical law was a preparation for the introduction of life. The conception of causality as employed in the physical sciences does not require a scientist to say more than that there are certain fixed conditions under which all the changes in the world take place. It is certainly a great gain to know the fixed conditions under which changes take place, and we rejoice to know these. When, however, following out the changes that take place under these fixed conditions, and tracing out these changes themselves, we find that they converge toward a fixed point, what are we to say? May we not go back and read the story again with a fresh light, and from a new point of view? The fixed conditions under which all changes take place are themselves indicative of intelligence, all we do when we regard the changes from the new point of view is simply to enhance our idea of the character of the intelligence that causes these fixed conditions to converge toward a predetermined end.

The question of a predetermined end might have been raised at almost any point in the story which science tells of the making of the worlds, but to raise it then and there would not have added to the clearness of the issue. It seems best to raise it at the point where, in the history of time and time's changes, the great transition from non-living to living matter took place. For with the introduction of life the terminology of science, and the conceptions with which science works, necessarily change. From this time onwards purpose is in evidence, and the language descriptive of changes in living matter, even when used by those who profess to think that such changes are ultimately mechanical, is full of indications of purpose. Now it is not well to split nature up into compartments, or to fill it with distinctions which seem to shut one part out from relation to another part, and therefore we take our stand on the conception that even, in that part of nature which seems under the domain of mechanical law, purpose is not excluded. Mechanical law is the way whereby purpose realizes its end. In our own experience necessity is the presupposition of freedom. Assuming at this stage of our argument that freedom is possible, then we say that it is possible only in a world ruled according to fixed laws, and which changes under fixed conditions. Speech is possible because of the fact that words have definite meanings, and because language has determined laws of construction. I say nothing of other fixed conditions, such as the laws of acoustics and so on, which are also necessary conditions for the possibility of communication from man to man. To this I may return later on, and in other connections; I make the remark here to show that the fixed necessities which can be expressed in mechanical law are both the presupposition of purpose and the means by which purpose is realized.

Thus we do not interfere, in any way, with the work or the method of mechanical science, when we take their results and show that they may be read in another fashion. Nor do we bring to the reading of their results any new or unheard-of principle. We are simply doing what, in other spheres of thought, we do every day. Nor is it contended that it would be wise or safe to take the idea of purpose as a clew to guide us in the investigation of physical phenomena. There are many considerations which warn us that such a clew might lead astray, and be unfruitful. The main reason is our ignorance, and our tendency to see purpose where we cannot give any satisfactory reason for its existence. But surely that is no reason why we should refuse to recognize purpose, when it is almost forced on us by science itself. The very fact that we are suspicious of final causes, and that we rigidly exclude the thought of them in physical investigation, ought to enable us to recognize them with all promptness, when they present themselves to us as the outcome of a series of physical investigations conducted without regard to them, from which they were altogether excluded.

Such seems to be the case with the convergence of causes, which brought about the introduction of life on this globe. We are driven to the conclusion that this was no accident, but the outcome of a long series of preparations, and that it was meant. There can be no controversy as to the convergence of conditions. No one lays more stress on this than the evolutionist, or even the mechanical evolutionist, who attempts to set forth evolution as a distribution of matter and motion. Accepting the accounts of the distribution and redistribution of matter and motion, we see that the process of distribution had proceeded very far, and differentiation and integration had run their course for a very lengthened period before things were ripe for the advent of life.

I do not lay stress here on the mere fact of this fresh departure. I do not ask science to account for the origin of life, for I should be told that science has nothing to do with origins. Nor do I care to rest the theistic argument on origins alone. For if I cannot find the Divine Being in what is fixed, stated, settled, I fear I shall not find Him anywhere. Clearly, however, he who believes in intelligence and power, as being at the basis of things, is not in the same position, in the presence of new departures, as he is who has undertaken to account for all things by means of principles, which he has known only in connection with the world as it was before the new departure was taken. It means that up to the point at which life entered into the world, science had no reason to widen its conception of the world so as to recognize the conception of life. It did not need to recognize organization, or organic relations in its conception of being. Being as conservative as are all the attitudes of the human mind, science is unwilling to widen its conceptions, or recognize the need of coördinating its notions — with conservative energy it has clung to the desire to make its old machinery cope with the new problem. Hence the efforts, which we make free to call despairing efforts, to reduce the facts of life to such a minimum as would make methods of physics and chemistry adequate to their explanation. The phenomena of life, it is contended, must be explicable by the principles of physics and chemistry. Did not inorganic existence precede organic existence? was there not a time when life was not? Now life is; and must not life be the product of inorganic existence?

It is not necessary to enter deeply into the dead controversy about the origin of life. I am old enough to remember the shout of triumph which arose when an experimenter declared that he had seen the rise of living from non-living matter, and the consequent gladness of those who desired to exclude the recognition of forces other than those which were physical and chemical. Nor can one remember, without a smile, the short-lived Bathybius. Speedily it turned out that the spontaneous generation of Dr. Bastian's bacteria arose, not from non-living matter, but from infusions imperfectly sterilized, and nowadays it is the sure conviction of science that life comes only from life. Still the longing to believe the opposite lingers, and now the wish to believe takes the form of an inverted prediction, that is a prediction not with respect to the future, but with respect to the past, that if the gentleman, who wishes to believe, had lived at the time when life appeared, he would expect to see it evolve from non-living matter. At all events, the transition of non-living into living matter, without the intervention of life, does not belong to our era.

"What is implied in the origination of life is not that inorganic nature produced life, but that a new form of existence presented itself at a certain period of time in the history of the earth. But this life, although it has for the first time presented itself, is not something that has come into being by a power belonging to inorganic things. And no one would be so absurd as to say that it originated from itself. Its origination can be explained only on the supposition that it was implicit in the nature of existence *as a whole*. Outside of the unity that comprehends all possible existence, there is nothing; and therefore life, when it appears, merely manifests in an explicit form what was already wrapped up in the one single existence that is manifested in all modes of existence. But, if this one all-inclusive unity is now seen to involve within itself organic as well as inorganic existence, its nature cannot be comprehended by looking at either apart from the other. It is neither inorganic nor organic, but both. Further, it implies that organic existence is of this nature that, while it contains all that is implied in inorganic nature, it also manifests characteristics that are peculiar to itself." ("Outline of Philosophy," by Professor Watson, p. 181.) The paragraph from Dr. Watson expressed my meaning so exactly that I could not help appropriating it. Yet I do not commit myself to all that is implied in it, for the passage quoted is organically related to a whole system of philosophy, which I do not hold in all its implications. I quote it, therefore, without prejudice. I agree with it in saying that life cannot be derived from inorganic matter, and also in the implication that the intelligent ground of the world must be a living power; what further is to be said will appear in due time.

Meanwhile let us look at the world as it appears under the light shed on it by this fresh appearance. From the scientific point of view the contrast between living and non-living matter has been made the ground for the division of the natural sciences into two great groups, known as the biological and the physical sciences. Here we have to do with matter which has entered into a peculiar state or condition. Without entering into the vexed question of the existence of vital force, or claiming a distinctive existence of vitalism, we may at least point out that matter takes on new forms and peculiar properties which are not found in inorganic matter. These properties are still properties of matter, and many claim that they can be explained mechanically. Professor Huxley said in his Belfast address (1874), "In the seventeenth century the idea that the physical processes of life are capable of being explained in the same way as other physical phenomena, and, therefore, that the living body is a mechanism, was proved to be true for certain classes of vital action; and, having thus taken firm root in irrefragable fact, this conception has not only successfully repelled every assault which has been made upon it, but has steadily grown in force and extent of application until it is now the expressed or implied fundamental proposition of the whole doctrine of scientific physiology." It is evident that Professor Huxley uses the word "mechanism" in a wider sense than that which the word has in physics. If it be a mechanism, it is one of a peculiar kind. For Huxley, speaking when he was not on the war-path, uses words which concede all that we need for the great distinction between living and lifeless matter. Speaking of the distinctive properties of living matter, he says, "Its chemical composition containing, as it invariably does, one or more forms of a complex compound of carbon, hydrogen, oxygen, and nitrogen, the so-called protein (which has never yet been obtained except as a product of living bodies) united with a large proportion of water, and forming the chief constituent of a substance which, in its primary unmodified state is known as proto-plasm." ("Encyclopædia Britannica," art. *Biology*.) All that is needed is contained in the statement within brackets, in the foregoing quotation, namely, that protein has never been obtained except as a product of living bodies. It is open to the inorganic chemist to insist on the properties of the various elements which are found in protein; he may point out the vigorous combining power of oxygen, the inertia of nitrogen, the great molecular mobility of hydrogen, and the allotropic properties of carbon, sulphur, and phosphorus, as has been done by Mr. Herbert Spencer is his "Principles of Biology," and it may be shown that all these are of significance when considered as properties of living matter; but the fact remains that these properties remained hidden until they were revealed by the touch of life.

Taking at present only that feature of life which deals with the chemical composition of living matter, we see that life has revealed to chemists a new domain. It is easily understood how reluctant they would be to recognize something involving facts and principles which they had not seen while dealing with inorganic matter. We can sympathize with them in their efforts to build up without the aid of life those compounds which are the usual products of living bodies. In some respects they appear to have been successful, but they accomplish at great cost and labour and with many appliances what life is doing easily every moment. The success has not as yet been very great. Even were it more successful the result would have little bearing on the controversy between vitalism and non-vitalism. It is well to be assured that life has no substance peculiar to itself, and that every element found in living matter is found also in lifeless matter. It is well to know that living matter is subject to all the physical conditions which obtain in body as such. It is subject to gravitation, it exists only within certain limits of temperature, it breathes, when it does breathe, in accordance with laws of gaseous diffusion, and in fact the laws of physics and chemistry are operative on the matter which is living as on matter which is dead. For all these facts assure us that we are in one world, and that the organic and inorganic are most intimately related to one another.

It is not to be denied that the advent of life revealed within the world of matter new possibilities, and achieved positive results of the most wonderful kind. Without the introduction of anything new in the way of chemical elements, or without drawing on any physical force unknown, or unused in physics, it has seized the elements and transformed them, lifted them to a higher level, and sent them forth to new issues. How it has done it we may faintly guess, but we do not know. Certainly we shall never know if we stubbornly refuse to recognize that we are unable to explain them by the methods and assumptions which we found adequate in other spheres.

Life enters into the world and suddenly the world takes on a new meaning. The elements seem to recognize the hand of a master and quietly assume new combinations, enter on new forms, obey new laws, and begin a new course of evolution. Not only does it teach to chemistry a new series of lessons, and give to physics new meanings, it opens to us a new world for the understanding of which we must learn a number of new conceptions. Living matter does not only contain those peculiar bodies which we call proteids, it has the power of manufacturing them out of other substances. Every living organism is a stream into which a number of elements of matter constantly flow in, and a number as constantly flow out. But the inflow and outflow are arranged so as to be kept from any interference with the identity of the organism. The material particles of the organism are never the same at any two moments; the organism is one and the same throughout all its history. Moment by moment it is being disintegrated, and moment by moment it is renewed by the taking in of new matter which it raises to a level fit for its use. Thus in a constant series of changes it maintains its identity, and keeps up its correspondence with its environment. Clearly here we have to do not with the composition of forces and a resultant. Pressure

E

from behind and movement in the line of least resistance will not avail toward the complicated movement of a living organism, however simple it may be. Nor will it help us to call to our aid the behaviour of crystals, however beautiful and wonderful they may be. For crystals grow, if growth be a proper description of the process, by accretion from without, and the matter of crystals undergoes no modification as it is laid down according to the pattern of each kind of crystal. In an organism the matter is not added from without, but taken within, and made to undergo a process of union and differentiation until it becomes like the molecules it replaces.

When we read the description of the behaviour of living bodies by those who know, and specially when they are simply describing them without a controversial aim, we see that they describe them as if the chemical elements obeyed a new law, and were constrained to a new service. Sometimes it is said, as by Huxley, that "oxygen seizes on those organic molecules that are disposable, lays hold on their elements, and combines with them into the new and stabler forms, carbonic acid, water, and urea." This was only a way of putting the matter which has been departed from by more recent science which has seen it to be far from a real description of what happens. The relations between oxidation and life seem to be more complicated. Oxygen does not lay hold, but is itself laid hold of, and is disposed according to the needs of the organism. It may be simply handed or forced onwards by the living cells which grasp it. The living cell, and not the amount of oxygen in the blood, regulates the consumption of oxygen. As with oxygen so with all other elements that enter into the structure of living bodies. As soon as they enter into the service of life, they are acted on in new ways, made part of the organic system, and are kept in that service while they form part of the organism. The freedom of the molecules and their return to their simplicity and relative independence come with the dissolution of the organism, or with the release of the molecule from any connection with the organism.

For any proper understanding of the organism we must accept the assumption of the unity of the organism. We start not from physics, nor from chemistry, but from a conception that recognizes the unity of the organism as a whole made up of many related parts, each of which has meaning only in relation to all the others and to the whole. Any description of life involves this, and we must just accept life as given, and be content though we are unable to derive it from non-living matter. Spencer has said, "We find it impossible to think of life as imported into the unit of protoplasm from without; and yet we find it impossible to conceive it as emerging from the coöperation of the elements." ("Principles of Biology," Vol. I., p. 122, edition 1898.)

We may accept his testimony to the conclusion that we are unable to conceive life as a resultant of the components, and we may find it difficult to think of life as an addition from without, and yet dissent from his peculiar theory of metaphysics, and his frequent reference to "alternate impossibilities of thought." It is scarcely open to any one but himself to keep the unknowable as a convenient storehouse for the warehousing of difficult problems. His followers have ever sought to reduce the number of unknowables which he has laid up in store, and some of them are impatient with the great "unknowable," the father of all the smaller unknowables which appear in the Synthetic Philosophy. In the present instance, however, we can agree with him that we cannot conceive the unity of the organism as emerging from the coöperation of the elements. Nor can we conceive it as the result of any action of the parts. It is curious to find how many of the teachers of biological science are unwilling frankly to accept the unity of the organism as ultimate.

To discuss all the questions that arise in connection with the conception of the unity of the organism would lead us very far afield. The metaphysics of biology is something wonderful, equalled only by the metaphysics of physical science. We cannot discuss it here. Biologists seem always to strive after a derivation of the unity of a living organism. Research seems to give us an organism that works together, that holds many qualities together in the doing of work, and biology strives to account for the origin of the unity. Biologists reduce it to a unity of quality, or they postulate some agent to the working of which they ascribe the unity which is present to their observation, or they split up the unity of the organism and place a number of elements in mere external relation to the organism, and wander about in hopeless attempts to restore the lost unity.

It would seem, therefore, that in presence of the phenomena of life we ought to widen our conceptions, or, rather, we ought to form new conceptions applicable to a new form of experience. We ought to learn that there is a wider sense of unity than that which we learned in connection with our experience of the world without life. An abstract unity was, for the most part, quite sufficient for our purpose in dealing with problems of physics or chemistry. No doubt in chemistry we had to learn that two and two did not always make four, sometimes they made one. We learned also that a number of separate elements, sometimes a large number, come together to make one. But it was still possible to consider that the unity was constituted by the coöperation of the parts. It did tax our power of conception to think them so, and it was difficult to think of the chemical fact that a number of elements present in the compound in exactly the same proportions, and in the same quantities, should produce bodies so unlike as they some-

times do. The facts of isomerism show that this is so.
Thus gradually we came to attach a wider meaning
to unity. Then came life to give us a still wider conception to unity, that is, if we are to be true to the
facts of the case.   Now we have to learn to think of
a unity holding together many elements in a system,
maintaining that unity while the materials compos-
ing it come and go, maintaining that unity in the
midst of changes within itself and in relation to its
environment, and able not only to maintain itself but
to reproduce other organisms after its likeness.

To take into our minds the possibility of such a
unity as we have described indicated a great advance
in our power of thought. And I for one do not
wonder that men have found it difficult to make the
advance. There were difficulties from the side of
science, and difficulties from the side of metaphysics.
Science was unwilling to widen its terms, and metaphysics was unwilling to admit the possibility of a
unity that was not absolute, or rather to admit any
unity save that of the absolute. The metaphysical
difficulties have found expression in Mr. Bradley's
"Appearance and Reality." Without entering into
the metaphysical difficulties at this time, we may say
that, so far at least as biology is concerned, we must
learn to think in conceptions which, as far as possible, will grasp the real ongoing of that about which
we think. We must think of a unity, the parts of
which are what they are only in relation to one

another and to the whole. It is not allowable to take one in abstraction from another, or to think of it as if independent. We may try to do so if we please, but at the cost of moving away from the concrete reality which we seek to understand. We may speak, if we choose, of an environment and of an organism, and speak of them as brought together, but we must constantly remind ourselves that this is only our way of speaking, for these are only given in relation to one another. We may also speak of parts of the organism, and break it up into aspects, but that again is only our way of speaking, and we have to strive to think things together, as we find them exist together in our experience.

When we have won this new experience, and have widened our notions to correspond, we go back to look at the universe in a new light. It is a universe of a new kind containing in it a kind of existence not recognized before. It is also a universe that has made a greater demand on our intelligence, and called for a greater intellectual effort to understand it. The ongoing of it is more complex, and the wonder of it infinitely greater. Also the relative independence of what is in the world is greater. Here is something that lives, maintains itself, subdues alien matter, and turns it to its own uses, that grows, and produces other things that live and grow, which is so made that it is made to make itself. Its maintenance depends on its own activity. Shall we not say that this is a greater world than that disclosed to us in the worlds revealed to us in all the sidereal heavens? If quality rather than bulk is to be our criterion, then the smallest speck of life may have more significance than a world of lifeless matter. It was customary not long ago to speak of the structureless cell as the characteristic of living matter. All living animals, it was found, could be traced back to a single cell, and from this cell by repeated division all the component cells are derived. It was also found that certain animals remain single cells all their lives, and others became multicellular, and this evidently is one of the most important distinctions in zoölogy. It was thought that it was easier to bring zoölogical phenomena under the general conception of evolution if a beginning was made from the simplicity of a structureless cell, and by successive differentiations and integrations follow its growth until it arrived at the adult stage. But a change has come over the spirit of that dream. The structureless cell has vanished, and recent investigation reveals innumerable complexities even within the single-celled animal.

Our present interest in the cell theory is not to describe it, even in the most general terms, but to take that which lies at the very beginning of life, the single cell, and to see what a problem it is to think it. We may take from a master in this department of science the following: "It would appear from these more recent researches, of which time has only permitted me to give a brief and most imperfect summary, that the cell theory, great and important as it is most undoubtedly, is rather the commencement of a great movement, a fresh starting-point from which to begin investigations anew, than a complete scheme, or final explanation; and the one great lesson for us to learn is that processes of apparently the simplest kind are really of an extremely complicated nature, and will well repay the most minute and attentive study; for a right understanding of the changes that occur during the act of division of an ordinary epithelial cell, and of the causes determining those changes, would throw most welcome light on the more complicated processes accompanying the ripening and fertilization of the egg, which microscopists of all nationalities are at present studying with such intense earnestness." (" Biological Lectures," by Arthur Milnes Marshall, pp. 190-1.) Thus if we look at the simple cell as it is in itself at the earliest moment, we see a most complicated structure, and the structure is held together in a unity. When we have regard to its life history and to the changes through which it passes in the course of its growth, — and all these changes have also to be regarded as a unity, — then we would do well to revise our conception of a unity and its possibilities.

These qualities, relations, processes, are there as one, and it would be well for us to recognize them as one. If our thinking is to have a relation to reality, we must not substitute a mere aspect of the whole for the complicated process which actually goes on. The mere word "cell" must not take the place of the fact, nor ought we to break up the fact into a number of separate processes, select one of these as cause, and make the other results of that one we perhaps selected in a somewhat arbitrary way; for the cell is there with so many relations, qualities, properties, all belonging together, and forming a real unity. We shall find as we proceed that we are under the necessity of enlarging our conceptions of a unity, and we shall be under the necessity of thinking, or trying to think, of the many in the light of one. That is actually what nature is doing, and we must remind ourselves of the fact, if we are to understand nature. Thus we dwell on the simplest form of life, and speak of it even to weariness, just to make ourselves realize how great is the problem that it represents to our thought.

If we have been able to think a single cell in its isolation, its simplicity, and complexity, we must remember that we have done so by a process of abstraction. We neglected everything, and fixed our attention on the single cell. That is to say, we neglected its relation to the environment, the conditions of the world which made its existence possible as a living cell, the past history of time and its changes, and before our thinking could represent the reality these relations should be restored. But things are so in their reality, they are placed so in time and space, and are so related to all else that the history of a single cell implies the former history of the universe. We toil after this in vain, but even the distant glimpses we obtain of reality suggest that there is a thinker whose intellectual processes are adequate to the perfect understanding of the universe as it is, and as it works.

Looking at the universe from the point of view we have now attained, we see it is a unity which has life in it. We see also that, while we may think of the cell in abstraction, we are immediately reminded that the abstraction is ours. The life of the cell is in relation to the whole, and is one phase of the life that is in existence. And the world as a whole is something more than a system of mechanical forces, it has in it the principle of life. As our argument unfolds itself we shall see how much is implied in this great fact. We shall find in connection with life as it unfolds itself within the world, there are many new qualities brought within our view, which will help us to know something of the nature of the living power which, so far, we have already come to know. We have seen that the world is both organic and inorganic, and that these are one world, not tied together merely as cause and effect, but standing in reciprocal relation to one another. The advent of life is an unveiling of the power that is at work in the world, and if in its simplest form life presents so grave a problem to our intelligence, what will the fulness of life present to our view? We may not answer that question at this stage, but we may again lay stress on the fact that the advent of life has made known to us a new world, and a world that has brought with it its own method and action, and calls on us to meet it with a widening of our methods and actions if our intelligence is to keep pace with the working of the world.

The one cell which remains a single cell through its life history has already presented us with problems sufficiently hard and perplexing. What shall we then say of the advance from unicellular to multicellular being, which has been called one of the most important and significant steps taken by living being? The single cell which, be its origin what it may, proceeds on its course, passes beyond the stage of selfhood, and becomes a being of many cells. By modifications of itself, by splitting up into many cells, it grows ever more and more complex. It sets particular cells to specific work. It differentiates the structure so as to make each structure fit for certain functions. Some become bone cells, some muscles; some assume one form, some another, for the division is endless. I do not enumerate them, as they are accessible to every one, and my purpose is not to set forth the details, but to look at them in the light they cast on our thesis. As we pass from the being of one cell to the being formed of many cells, differentiated and integrated to meet a larger purpose, we pass from the thought of a unity of comparatively simple functions to one of a very great complexity. It is as if we passed from the study of a single individual to the study of a community made up of many individuals. All the individuals are of the same kind, and arise in the same way from modifications of the original cell, but they become most diverse in kind, and perform functions of the most unlike order. While each one of the number becomes what it is, and sets itself to its own individual work, it lives and acts in harmony with all the others, and in subordination to the whole organism. There is no community so well-ordered, so law-abiding, as is the community of cells which makes up the substance of a healthy organism.

As we follow on in our thought the history of the organism, we see other facts quite as striking. It is not merely a community of cells working together that we see, it is a community the individual members of which are ever changing. The cells, or the matter of which they are composed, pass and a new set takes their place. The organism is ever preparing, out of matter which it assimilates, the new cells which take the place of the old whose energy has been expended in doing the work of the organism, and the new cells seem to serve themselves heirs to the experience of the old, and the work goes on.

The process of training seems to be very speedily accomplished, for in this institution there seem to be no dull or self-willed pupils.

Not only has the organism the property of making alien matter a part of itself, and of making it serve the purposes of the organism, but there are even more surprising transformations still. Hitherto we have looked at the organism as a unity that maintains itself, sustains itself, and holds itself together during the time of its life history. We must look at it from another side. For we find that it has established certain fixed ways of communication with the environment, and these ways are made by a specialization of its own substance. One of these ways was implied in what was said when we spoke of its power of taking in alien matter and transforming it to its own uses. There are ways of which we have not yet spoken which enhance our conception of the vast complexity of an organism. It lays hold of the rays of light and transforms the undulations of the ether into a subjective state which we call vision. It seizes the vibrations of the atmosphere, and they, also, take a subjective form, and sound becomes hearing. It recognizes tastes, smells, resistance, and these external movements are turned into something altogether different, and yet related to the qualities of the environment so that these subjective states are a guide to the action which the organism should take for its own maintenance. Still further these inner states of the organism, related to states of the environment, give rise to something which seems to have no correspondence to anything outside of the organism. Sensations which are related to particular states of certain definite organs can be understood by reference to a definite organ of sense. But there is feeling which seems to need no definite organ for its existence; it is neither sight, taste, touch, smell, nor hearing, it is localized nowhere; as Sir William Hamilton said, it is subjectively subjective.

Without entering into the psychology of feeling here, — confessedly the most difficult question in psychology, — it is sufficient for me at present to call attention to the fact that feeling seems to be the accompaniment of life, if not universally, at least of life which has attained a certain measure of organization. We have therefore to add to our view of organization this subjective side in order to have a view of the manifoldness of this unity. It cannot be understood; it cannot, even, be stated, without a reference to purpose. For the biologist always speaks of the organism as adapted to the end of living, as surviving in the struggle for existence, and in so doing he has given it a meaning other than that which belongs to a series of physical processes. Such teleological references imply feeling, and effort, and impulse as the result of feeling. It may be that the explanation of the maintenance and striving of the organism does not admit of explanation without a reference to the subjective state of feeling, which is the source of all its effort. At all events there must be a centre to which all the states of the organism must be referred, and from which all its actions go forth.

We have come thus far under the guidance of science. We see an organism at work, we see it making use of the environment for its own purpose, we see it holding together the various elements of matter of which materially it is composed, keeping them under its control while they are in its service, and as we turn to the inward condition of the organism itself, we see a new, subjective world of sensation and feeling unlike anything which we found in the world of matter or even in the lower forms of life. At all events if feeling is in the lower forms of life it is so feebly manifested that we are unable to recognize it. So we come to the conclusion that this is a universe in which there is not only power, intelligence, life, but we are able to recognize that there is feeling in the universe. Again, we must widen our conception of reality, and call on thought for a greater effort than before, if our thought is to grasp reality. As yet we may not be able to interpret rightly the phenomena of power, intelligence, life, or feeling which have met our view as we ascended the stream of a developing universe. We may need a principle of interpretation which has not yet been manifested, but at all events we see so far the facts which need explanation. We may not understand feeling till we see it as it exists in a self-conscious being, or any principle of the lower world until we see it in its highest relations. The source of explanation and the principle of explanation may not lie in the beginnings of things, but in the end. However that may be, let us recognize what has been found by us up to this point, and follow on to the larger issues yet to come.

F

III

LIFE: ITS GENESIS, GROWTH, AND MEANING

To enable us to realize the complexity of an organism, we have only to recall the fact that naturalists are constrained not only to speak of the whole system of a living being, but also of a number of systems within that system. They speak of the alimentary, the circulatory, the nervous, the motor, the sensitive, and the reproductive systems. Each of these is sufficiently definite to demand a separate treatment. Each, also, has a distinctive character, and as set forth in the text-books one is apt to forget its relation to the other systems with which it is coördinated in the unity of the organism. At the conclusion of the section on the structure of living things Messrs. Sedgwick and Wilson say: "Up to this point we have considered living organisms from an anatomical and analytical standpoint, and have observed their natural subdivisions into organs, tissues, and cells. We have now only to remark that these parts are mutually interdependent, and that the organism as a whole is greater than any of its parts. Precisely as a chronometer is superior to an aggregate of wheels and springs, so a living organism is superior in the solidarity of its parts to a mere aggregate of organs, tissues, and cells." (Sedgwick and Wilson's "Introduction to General Biology," 2d edition, p. 19.) Again: "The process of cell division does not in this case go so far as complete cell separation, and the cells do not acquire a complete individuality. They do, it is true, acquire a certain independence of structure and function ; and their individual characteristics may even depart widely from those of neighbouring cells. Nevertheless they remain closely united by either material or physiological bonds to form one body. The body is not, however, to be regarded as merely an assemblage of independent, individual cells. THE BODY IS THE INDIVIDUAL; its more or less perfect division into cells is only a basis for the physiological division of labour, of which cell differentiation is the outward expression." (p. 156.)

In this singularly able and instructive book we find stress laid on the unity of the organism, and those who study biology from a wider view than the biological find themselves greatly helped by the distinguished authors. At all events my own debt of gratitude to them is great. I needed help to think the organism, and help was sought by me from all sources, and I was not able to see the manifold reflected into unity till I read the book to which I refer. They enabled me to see that the body is the individual, and the unity of the body is not to be lost sight

of in the multiplicity of details. It is not explained
by the coöperation of the parts, rather it is the explanation of them. The meaning of a unity is thus
growing on our hands, and the end is not yet ; it will
grow to larger issues still. Meanwhile we look at it
once more, and we see not merely a series of cells
in constant movement and change, but we see system
within system, or system beside system, all working
together in harmonious order, and all the systems
have a meaning only in relation to the system of the
whole of which they form a part, and which is more
than the sum of them all. The adequate way of
treating the organism would be to think it together,
even as, in fact, it is held together in actual existence.
This may be too great a task for our power of thinking, but it is a task which has been done. A thought,
an idea, is in the organism, for the organism is there,
exists in its manifoldness and unity, as an actual fact
in this world of space and time. If we cannot grasp
it in its greatness, at least let us acknowledge it as
a goal to our thought, and seek to grasp it at least
in outline.

One does not find much help from the authorities
on biology in the attempt to think the organism in
its unity, nor much practical recognition of the unity
of the organism. Rather we find a constant attempt
to evade the difficulty of the problem and a tendency
to substitute something more easily grasped. Huxley
calls the body "an aggregation of quasi-indepen-

dent cells," and Virchow says "the organism is not a unity, but is a company or rather a society." And Professor Geddes says, " For actual biological purposes the life of an organism is the sum of its functions, internal and external." (" Chambers's Encyclopædia," art. *Biology*.) The problem of life is attacked now from the side of the cell, now from the tissue, and again from the protoplasm, and the point of view varies according to the aspect in which it is viewed. But from biologists generally we get but little help in our desire to study the individual as a unity. Every theory seems to move by the disintegration of the individual into self-efficient and unrelated parts. Sometimes these are physical or chemical elements, sometimes a company of cells, and sometimes physiological units. So much stress is laid on the similarity, and on the independence of cells, that the individual disappears. The true individuals appear to be the cells, and the organism seems to be explained as a result of the behaviour of the cells as they grow, reproduce, and differentiate themselves. But the relation of whole and part cannot be studied by the microscope. If we are to get at the secret of the organism, we must study it in relation to the organism, and look at all the qualities as properties of the organism. "Of this organization itself as such — that is, of the mechanical apparatus it presents to us — the microscope tells us nothing whatever. The microscope only enables us

to see a single cell, a single germinal particle in connection with more or less of its own formed material
—a single coral, so to speak, and the polype that
died into it; it tells us nothing whatever of the vast
machine which these polypes have all unconsciously
built up with their coral. The mighty and complex
frame of man is, after all, despite its innumerable
parts, a unity; all these parts but go toward that unity,
are sublated into it. Now, what of all that does microscopic observation tell us? Why, simply nothing.
Myriads of miserable Egyptians carried stones to
the pyramid, but no microscopic watching of any of
these, stone and all, would ever explain the pyramid
itself—its many to a one." (Hutchison Stirling,
" As Regards Protoplasm," p. 75.)

The substitution of the idea of a community for
that of a unity seems to give an easier problem for
solution, because a community is thought of as a
loose and apparently fortuitous concourse of individuals, each independent of all the others. Whether
society can be regarded as a crowd and not as a real
unity is another question on which something may be
said later, but from a certain standpoint society may
be looked at as a crowd of independent or quasiindependent units. If this is the sense attached to
the term, it is a term quite inadequate to express the
unity of the body, and can only mislead. For biology
it may suffice to say that the life of an organism is
the sum of its functions, but for real thought the

organism is more than a sum. It is something that holds together the whole ongoing of the organic qualities, functions, etc., and makes them work together for the aims and purposes of the organism. Every cell, while it is within the body, is in the service of the organism, and its modifications, its changes, its food, its waste, its very form, are determined for it by the whole. It is maintained only while it is within the body, when removed from the organism it perishes and passes to a lower chemical condition.

Thus, also, we must think of the variations to which the organism is subject. They cannot be arbitrary nor can they be unlimited. For the organism is so tied together that a variation in one part gives rise to a number of correlated variations so great as to be beyond reckoning. The supposition of innumerable variations is a hypothesis that has bulked largely in the theory of evolution, and it seems to me to be greatly exaggerated. Confining our view to a single organism, it certainly does not admit of indefinite variation. It is not my intention, however, to criticise the adequacy of the multitudinous machinery which has been invented to make the theory of evolution intelligible. For from my point of view, at present, I have no interest in such criticism. I am willing to accept the fact of evolution, though I do not think the factors of evolution have been discovered as yet. We know that life appeared on the earth in a simple form, that it proceeded in forms which grew from more to more, that there is a gradation and a sequence in the appearance of life on the earth, and that the latest form of life is the highest form that has yet appeared. So far agreement reigns; further agreement may be attained if we say that each lower form of life precedes the higher in point of time, in order of organization, and, perhaps, also in causal preparation. It may be that each form was evolved from a lower by successive modifications, and that all forms of life are organically and causally connected with the first forms which appeared. Species may be not fixed and unchangeable, but subject to a law of progress and change. If this be so, all the reference it has to my argument is to make me widen my view of unity, and to call on me to grasp, if I can, a larger manifold in a single unity. It has been difficult enough to grasp the conception of a single organism, so complex have we found it to be. We have found also that we were ever trying to substitute an abstract conception for the concrete reality. To what straits shall we be driven when we find ourselves in the presence of a vast reality persisting through the ages, growing, changing, ever in adaptation with its environment, yet ever fixing itself in relatively permanent forms, and always in active movement. We might predict that we shall have a larger crop of abstractions than before, since the phenomena are more complex. And so we have. Heredity, variation, the struggle for existence, natural selection, the survival of the fittest, and a number of other phrases appear, some of which have passed into common speech.

As I said, I am not concerned to criticise these terms and what they stand for, except so far as they have become the symbols of a mechanical evolution; and thus tend to make mind derivative and secondary. Some of them seem to be without meaning and some seem to be mere expressions. Take the survival of the fittest, and, looking at the world of life as it is to-day, ask what it means. It really tells us nothing, affords us no criterion of life, gives no intimation of progress. Everything that survives is the fittest whether it be a unicellular being, or multicellular; whether it be a degraded form, or a form that is in the exercise of all its functions, with all its structures perfect. It adds nothing to our knowledge, nor does it give us any insight into the meaning of the changes that life has passed through.

Natural selection seems to be a name for a vast complexity of conditions to which life is subject, and now one and again another is to the front as it is most needed. It has sometimes to become more particular, and becomes cell selection, physiological selection, sexual selection, germinal selection, as the more general formula becomes clearly inadequate for its purpose. It is applied, too, for the purpose of explaining the advance of life into higher forms. It cannot, at the same time, and with the same machinery, explain the persistency of the lower and the advent of the higher forms of life. If there is a struggle for existence among the lower forms of life, how is it that they remained the same for all time, made no change, and have had no variation so far as we know? If there is no struggle for existence among the lower organisms, there is an utter absence of the motive for change which underlies the Darwinian hypothesis. It does not seem possible to find occasion for any advance from the simplicity of the immortal single celled beings to the dangerous struggle for existence that, according to Darwin, awaits the higher organisms. The single cell has every advantage; it is first in the field, and it persists still. Why did some cells become multicellular? The Darwinian machinery is silent.

Many other things might be said of the inadequacy of natural selection. Indeed, many things have been said, and these have, for the most part, been ignored by the thorough-going advocates of natural selection. Though it has been clearly shown that natural selection cannot originate anything, yet men continue to speak as if natural selection could do this, that, and the other thing. Though it appears that its function is negative, the killing off of the unfit, yet positive functions of the most productive sort are ascribed to it. At one time, it is said, natural selection does produce species, and with the next breath it has to wait for the appearance of a variation on which it may work.

Some contend that natural selection is sufficient to account for the origin of species; some, that it has a place along with other factors in the development of new forms of life; and some say that its function is mainly negative, inhibiting certain departures from the type, and so it is a something that makes for the stability of species. But underlying all the variations of the meaning of natural selection is the conception of the struggle for existence and fortuitous variation in all directions. It is a grewsome picture that they present to us under the name "the struggle for existence," and the demand for variation is so extensive that to comply with it would land us in a world governed only by chance. To speak first of the struggle for existence, and to speak with all brevity. It is most extensive. It is a struggle between organism and organism, between species and species, and between species and environment in all cases. The parts of a creature are also represented as struggling with one another, one set of cells struggling against another set, and food for brain cells may mean lack of food for motor cells, and so on. The idea of struggle has been followed out in all directions, and there is no possible relation between one part of the body and another part, between one organism and another, between one species and another, but may easily be presented as a struggle. Struggle thus presented tends to become an empty form.

Of course it is quite easy to present things so, and it is as useless as it is easy. But the presentation of the struggle is possible because we first take out of their relations the beings which struggle, look at them abstractly, and then seek to conceive of them as struggling to get back into relations. But we do not find any being subsisting out of relation to other beings. Relations and conditions may be set forth as if they were a struggle, and, indeed, a goodly number of the pictures of struggle are just the relations in which the creature stands, and the conditions of its existence without which it could not be. Neglecting the other aspects of struggle, let us look at the main picture. It has never yet been shown that a species is more numerous than can be supported by its means of subsistence, and in fact it does not seem ever to approach the limit of its subsistence. Many imaginary features have been introduced into the picture. The life of a species is looked at as something that strives to expand in all directions, and this tendency to expansion tends to bring it into collision with other beings, and being brought into collision they strive for advantage, and the one that obtains the mastery obtains the prize. Every organism is thus on the watch for any modification which may give it the mastery, and having found the modification it perpetuates it. Such is the picture presented to us.

Of the struggle we shall only say that it is universal,

at least it is represented as if it were. But general laws do not account for particular effects. What is needed is a knowledge of the specific causes which here or there place a check on the expansion of a species, and this is what is never forthcoming. There must be limits to the increase of a species, and Mr. Darwin in this relation says, "If asked how this is, one immediately replies that it is determined by some slight difference in climate, food, or the number of the enemies; yet how rarely, if ever, we can point out the precise cause or manner of the check." It reminds us of the favourite argument of another evolutionist who when he is confronted with a change which he cannot particularly explain, says what has happened must have happened, otherwise force would have ceased to persist. Such an explanation is purely formal. If the struggle were a fact of natural history, it would be quite easy to point to the struggle, and to indicate in detail the precise cause or manner of the check.

Apart from its environment and the conditions of its existence a living creature is for us inconceivable. By turning the creature into an abstraction it is possible to represent it as struggling with its environment, but the relation to its environment is simply that which makes its life possible. Similarly we may make every relation in which it stands to other beings, and every quality it has, a symbol of the struggle. But these relations, conditions, qualities, may be presented, and more truly, from another point of view. All other existence is needed in order that this particular being should exist in this time, place, and in this particular form.   For this end the sun must shine, the rain must fall, seedtime and harvest, summer and winter, must come and go, the tides ebb and flow, the grass grow, and other living things labour that this form of being may have a life of its own. So easy is it to turn the struggle inside out, and turn it into a set of enabling conditions without which this form of life would not be possible.

As to the demand for indefinite variation which is necessary to provide the material on which natural selection may work, we need not say much about it. The time of such indefinite variation, if it ever was, is long past.   Living matter has been sorted into definite lots, and species has been pretty well fixed for a long time.   The limits of the variation are very definite as far as present species are concerned. Whales do not vary in the direction of feathers, nor do birds tend to vary in the direction of fins.   Variation might have been somewhat indefinite long ago, but species vary now only within very definite limits. In fact, variable life is in the same condition as the pre-chemical matter of Sir Norman Lockyer — it has all been worked up into definite forms.   Indeed, if it were not for the desire to avoid the introduction of anything like guidance into the conception of the causes which account for the phenomena of life, it would have been a more likely account of the facts to suppose that the variations were definite and not indefinite. That something like guidance is needed is very evident, and from one point of view natural selection gives that guidance; while, on the other hand, natural selection is itself nothing but a set of conditions which may be dealt with quantitatively and mechanically. It keeps the word of promise to the ear, by showing us a principle at work which seems to lead life on to greater and greater issues; it breaks the word of promise by showing us that any kind of guidance is altogether absent. Professor Poulton, in criticism of the hypothesis of physiological selection of the late Mr. Romanes, says (he is speaking of fertility and infertility): "Mutual infertility is due to a single and uniform constitution rigidly kept within the narrowest limits, while a minute change of constitution in any direction means infertility. Mutual infertility is, in fact, but the single external indication of numberless changes of constitution. The necessary precision of adjustment of the male to the female germ-substance is only kept up in the species by unremitting selection, and there is no cause for surprise that it should cease when selection is no longer forthcoming for its support." Again, "Mutual fertility depends upon the exact relationship of two extraordinarily complex bodies, the germ cells of male and female; it depends upon a reciprocal adjustment of almost infinite precision." ("Nature," December 8, 1898, p. 122.)

This is quoted in order that we may have a conception of the marvellous things done by natural selection. Adjustments are kept up by unremitting selection, and under that selection a "reciprocal adjustment of almost infinite precision" is accomplished. Yet there is no sufficient agency set forth by which this work of infinite precision can be done. When we ask what it is, we are presented with a bewildering variety of conditions, some of which are highly problematical, and most of them vague and indefinite. At one time the struggle is set forth as universal, and again it is intermittent, for Professor Poulton speaks of a state in which "selection is no longer forthcoming." An agency so vague, and so indefinite, which at one time acts, and at another time ceases to act, which is now set forth as a conservative agent, and again as the most active power in revolution, ought at any rate to be sufficiently described. And this, we submit, has never been done.

There is, indeed, a selective power in life, there is a power at work of almost infinite precision, there is unremitting selection in the maintenance of what is gained so that there may not be retrogression, and also unremitting attention to the movement of life in relation to wider unities and large meanings; but the question is, can you rationally predicate such qualities of a series or congeries of varying agencies hypostatized under the name of natural selection?

At no time in the history of thought, or in the history of science, has there been so much attention given to the magnificent adjustments of life and the infinite precision of every one of them. We may gratefully acknowledge our indebtedness to the advocates of organic evolution for the wonderful light they have cast on the unity of life and on its endless diversity. We gratefully acknowledge that they have enabled us to see a much more wonderful variety of adjustments than the older teleology ever dreamed of. They have constrained the older teleologists to admit that the notion of an external artificer is no longer adequate. We cannot now think of an organism being put together as a watch is. On the other hand, they must also admit the consequences of their own work. When they call attention to the infinite precision of the adjustments of life, and dwell on the unremitting selection they find at work, they cannot dwell to any purpose, as in other relations they do, on the wastefulness of life, nor compare the steps that led to an adjustment, to the process of firing a thousand shots at an object, and hitting it only once. Infinite precision in one point is scarcely consistent with such bad shooting.

It does not yet appear what mode of speech they ought to depart from. From one point of view such aimless shooting is essential to their theory. For on their view such profusion of experiments is necessary to afford them an occasion for hitting on that happy accident which has a chance of permanence. Nature tries and tries again, and after innumerable failures, hits on a success, and then she buries her failures and goes on her way rejoicing. We prefer to follow them as they point out the infinite precision of these adjustments; we decline to believe them when they say that these have emerged as the outcome of an infinite series of trials and errors. If these adjustments are there now in almost infinite precision, we naturally think that the steps which led up to them were not lacking in precision. If the outcome of the process is full of such wonderful interrelations as are described in every book that treats of evolution, surely we may infer that the processes are also intelligible.

At all events we are justified in withholding our assent to the production of a world of life, out of processes in which no intelligible process can be discovered, at least until we have overwhelming evidence for such a conception. Evidence is not likely to be forthcoming, for nature has buried her failures. Meanwhile, we follow the guidance of those who unfold for us the history of life, and we leave on one side all the machinery which they have manufactured for the purpose of explaining the progress of life and the origin of species. These two things are by no means organically united, and that hypothesis is not the only, or the best one, for the explanation of the facts.

Historically, then, life appears as a simple cell, and in that form it is recognized in those geological strata in which it first appeared. Life goes on and appears in more and more complex forms. It is not necessary to enumerate these. Nor is it needful to enumerate the systems of classification, nor the species which have appeared in the history of the earth. Soon living things appear in various forms which have a relative permanence, for some of the earlier forms are here at this hour. The persistence of the earlier species goes on side by side with the introduction of newer and more highly evolved species, until the tree of life puts forth its greatest and most evolved fruit. There is permanence, there is gradation, there is progress; and all these are combined in the view of life disclosed to us by evolution. As to the kinds of living beings recognized by zoölogists, we do not find agreement among them. "They all recognize," says Professor MacBride, "a certain number of phyla. Each phylum includes a group of animals about whose relation to one another no one entertains a doubt. Each zoölogist, however, has his own idea as to the relationship which the various phyla bear to one another." (Professor MacBride in Spencer's "Biology," Vol. I., p. 386, edition 1898.) He enumerates seventeen phyla from the protozoa up to the chordata, which last includes the vertebrata.

As we follow the description of the various phyla from the protozoa, both with regard to their peculiar characteristics, and with regard to the order of their appearance in time, we are struck with the contrast between the clear, sharp discrimination of each from each, and with the definiteness of this work; and on the other hand, with the vague speculative account of the manner of the origin of each phylum, and the causes of their modifications into the form they now have. In the one case we have to do with the intelligible marks and conditions of a definite existence, distinguished from all other indefinite modes of life; in the other with the attempt to derive conditioned existence from a congeries of accidents, which makes any ordered outcome unintelligible. One cannot make such a transition. From intelligible results one can argue only to intelligible causes and processes. But this is not the only sphere in which men strive to make non-intelligence do the work of intelligence.

Each order of being is presented to us as being with a determinate kind of existence, conditioned in time and place, definitely related to other beings of the same kind and of other kinds. There is nothing uncertain or indeterminate in their qualities, nor anything to indicate that they are the product of accidental combinations. It would require an extension of the calculus of probabilities, hopelessly beyond our reach, to calculate the chances of a transition from a sphere of accidental combinations to a sphere of definite determinate existence. That calculation has not been made, nor can it be made.

As we follow the stream of life, we pass from the relatively simple to the complex, and the greater the complexity the greater becomes the dependence of the parts each on each. Certain forms of life seem to have in every part the power to reproduce the whole, but the higher organisms have lost that power. A highly organized nation knows when it is beaten, a nation loosely held together may keep up a partisan warfare for years. Unicellular life is almost indestructible, organized life may be extinguished by a breath. Still, we do not obtain an adequate conception of life until we look at its highest development, and obtain some idea of how it came to be. With this thought there opens out before us a great and luminous conception which we may regard apart from the external machinery of evolution. The conception is that the history of each individual is the history of life up to the point at which the form of life to which it belonged appeared. There is sufficient truth in this conception for us to use it, though it has been stated far too absolutely. Recapitulation is a fact so far at least as regards all creatures that have an embryonic life. Whether it is true of larvæ is questioned. No doubt there are some omissions, and many steps seem to be shortened, and yet there is enough to enable us to say that life seems to remember the steps by which it climbed upwards to higher and higher ends. If the recapitulation has nothing accidental or tentative about it, have we any good reason to think that the steps recapitulated were accidental?

In the recapitulation, too, the organism outruns the original method. It sets to work prophetically, and forms organs to fit a medium with which it is to be in relation only in the future. It forms eyes for the light that they have never seen, and ears adapted to the vibrations which they have never heard. This fact, which Mr. Spencer calls preadaptation, reveals to us a striking peculiarity of life, however we may explain it. We referred to eyes and ears as instances of preadaptation, but the whole organism of all creatures that pass through an embryonic stage of life is formed and adapted to a medium in which they do not live at the time of their formation. There can be no thought of chance combinations producing so wonderful a relation.

Life, then, whether we look at it as manifested in the individual, or as manifested in all living things, presents us with a vast and wonderful system of thought. It presents definite qualities as it appears in its simplest form; it seems to proceed in orderly progression from stage to stage; and wherever we find it, it is in exact relation with preceding and succeeding forms of life; and in exact relation also, not with an abstract environment, but with surroundings as definite and conditioned as it is itself. Here is no abstract organism to be thrust into an abstract environment, to which it must respond by some variation which will enable the one to correspond to the other; what we everywhere have is a real and definite correspondence, established as the very condition of the existence of the creature. There are changes in both, and larger correspondences arise as life becomes wider and more definite. May we not postulate in life this power to adapt itself to the changing conditions of its existence, and postulate also that this power acts in a regular and orderly fashion? Why should we postulate a blind thrusting out of life in all directions, and leave the result to accident? That is not the way of the life we see around us on all sides. We see economy, thrift, ends accomplished at the smallest cost of matter and energy; and an exact and infinite precision in the adjustment of means to ends. If the life we see is so wise and provident, shall we suppose it to be ignorant and wasteful in those processes which we hardly know at all?

As my purpose is not to follow the growth of life as it has appeared in the history of time, but to learn what is the meaning of that history, I shall not enter into details. It has many riddles, and many mysteries, yet we may safely say that, looking to the record of it, there have been method, advance, progress.

It has grown, developed, and advanced as if it had been guided by a power, who foresaw the end from the beginning and took steps to accomplish that end. We may never be able to say definitely what were the ends of life, but we may say that there are ends. We may never know why life seems to lead up to a *cul-de-sac* as in the case of mollusca, insecta, arachnidæ, and crustacea, and apparently in other branches of the tree of life. Taking the tree in Spencer's " Biology," it looks as if life had set forth on an exploring voyage, and had come to a position from which there was no further advance. While advancing in part on the right and left, it also advanced on the central line, and through the ascending line of the vertebrata came at last to a form, in which it became conscious of itself and of its meaning.

This is a difficulty to any theory of life, as much to the evolutionist as to any other. For the evolutionist is bound on his theory to find a use for everything and an advantage to the possessor of every quality which life has, even to the spots on a peacock's tail. It has also to explain why the changes and variation, which led from the simplest form of life up to insects, ceased at that point on that line, and went no further. The question may be put to me, and I shall answer — I do not know. There may be reasons which are unknown to me, which may never be known to me. Be that as it may, enough is known to me of the wisdom of that power made manifest in the relations of living beings to enable me to trust that wisdom is manifested here also. Darwin has shown us the toils of the earth-worm in the service of the higher life; research may show us that these forms of life, which have stopped short at a certain stage of organization, as if no further advance could be made on that line, may be of indispensable service to those higher forms that reached their higher development on another line. Perhaps the work done by these could not be done by forms of life determined by another line of ascent. For the manifold forms of life seem to be a gigantic system of coöperation, in which each exists for all the others. Certainly there are many facts that seem to lead to that conclusion — facts set forth in a new and interesting form by Prince Kropotkin, Professor Geddes, and others, on which I cannot dwell here.

Apart, then, from the machinery of evolution and the difficulties which it brings with it, we have learned to look at life as one. It has a continued history. The first form is bound up with the latest outcome of life. The highest form of life is the epitome of the whole history of life, and all life as at present consti-tuted is united together by many bonds, some visible, and some invisible. This great thought we owe to organic evolution and its expounders. It looks much more of a rational scheme than that which our fathers learned from their scientific teachers. They thought of a series of unrelated, special creations, each special

creation being suddenly thrust into an environment.
(See Milton's description.) Creatures are made not
without their own coöperation, and they are made so
as to make themselves. This, also, we have learned
from evolution. Evolution has laid stress on the
striving of life after greater fulness, on the stern
grip of life on every advantage gained, and on the
readiness of life to press on to larger issues. Inheritance cannot be merely received by it, the heir must
be equal to the inheritance, or it will pass away. Inherited qualities are, in the most real sense, also
acquired, while acquired qualities are transmitted,
Weissmann notwithstanding. But it is not really of
importance for us to advert to that controversy,
which seems to be a somewhat idle one. For the
main impulse to the denial of the transmission of
acquired qualities arises from the attempt of Weissmann to substitute another unity for the unity of the
organism. But we pass it by at present.

Looking at life from the standpoint we have now
attained, we see a web of the greatest complexity.
We see growth, gradation, adaptation, preadaptation,
organization, means adapted to ends, and larger ends,
dimly arising before our view, as, under the prompting of evolution, men are pressing on to explore the
vistas which beckon them on. Without controversy
the unveiling of the processes of life has given us a
larger conception of the wisdom of the power at work
in the phenomena of life. Something was learned of

wisdom even when we looked at life from the external standpoint of Paley. It gave us a lofty conception of the skill of the artificer. For the machinery was so much more skilfully constructed than any machine made by man, that the wisdom of the human and the divine artificer could not be compared. Then there were machines that produced other machines, to speak of organisms as machines for a moment, and making better machines as time went on, so that the carpenter did not give us an unworthy conception of the matter so far as mere skill of adaptation and use were concerned. But even Paley felt that the carpenter theory was inadequate, and the use he made of the argument and illustration was to show that these skilful contrivances were not without an adequate cause.

The effect of evolution has been simply to transfer the cause from a mere external influence working from without to an immanent rational principle. The skill of the carpenter is now within the living creatures, and they work onward and upwards to the issues now becoming manifest to the beholder. At all events the wisdom and the skill are there, account for them as we may. They are connected, too, with the actual working of life as that is manifested in the living beings we see in the world. At present it is too early to ask if the living power we see at work in the world of life is also a transcendent power, which means something for itself. As far as we have yet looked at the world and the phenomena presented to us by it, we have no data even for the consideration of such a question. For we see that a world of inorganic phenomena has become a world of life, and the story of the inorganic world could be rationally read as the story of a preparation for life, and the story of life — its existence, growth, and progress — was a story of the interactions between life and its environment, so that we have not had cause, as yet, to raise the question of the ground of the world and the character of that ground, save in so far as it is intimated to us by the manifestations we have seen. We may obtain more light as we proceed; meanwhile it is evident that there is power at work greater than we can measure, that there is wisdom of the highest kind at work, and that power is not a stranger to life.

It is not an unknowable power, for it is a manifested power, and a power so far as it is manifested is known, or may be known. It may transcend in its greatness and excellence our capacity of knowledge, we may have to speak of it as unlimited, and may have to use all kinds of adjectives to negative any limits to the positive excellence of it, but negative adjectives do not alter the positive character of the power. Unlimited power is power, and endless life is life. It is one of the most curious freaks of metaphysics that a power manifested in the whole universe should be described as unknowable. Underlying such a conception must lurk a curious theory of substance and attributes, which can only regard attributes as a way of concealing the substance. Attributes reveal substance, they are the qualities which define it, show its way of being and working, and enable it to be known. This way of speech is forced on us, for, if we could, we should never speak in that way. For the way of speaking supposes that we can separate being from its modes of manifestation; we may speak of substance in that way, as speech is sometimes unreal, but substance without attributes is nothing, and is unthinkable.

Beings who think at all cannot place at the basis of all things an unthinkable or postulate irrationality as the ground of an intelligible universe. The world does appear to exist in relations that can be thought, and the operations of it correspond to those which thought establishes among its objects. At all events, evolutionary science has shown us such relations between the life of the present and the life of the past as to make the relation between them one that we can understand. If the advocates of evolution have postulated accidental causes, and done much to make the transition from the category of cause and effect to the category of means and end unthinkable, well, that is their misfortune, and may have arisen from inexact ways of thinking; but apart from that they have been successful in showing us a world of life which is intelligible. We take their results, and leave their philosophy on one side. We are grateful to them for enabling us to see that the world of life is a world governed by rational methods, and thus they have enabled us to say that there is a rational living power at work in the world. That is the only conclusion we infer at this stage.

As life unfolds itself, and as the possibilities of it come forth to view, other inferences may be drawn as to the character of the power at work in the universe, but we may not push any argument beyond its due limits. Only this we must say, that for purposes of rational explanation the highest and not the lowest is the standard of reference. If we are to explain the process of evolution, we must have regard, not to the starting-point, but to the goal. It is true that a hypothesis, precisely the opposite of this, lies at the basis of the synthetic philosophy of Mr. Herbert Spencer, and, also, at the basis of much current writing on evolutionary topics. This is the key to a great deal of their argumentation, and to their strenuous attempts to explain the higher in terms of the lower. One has sympathy with those who labour at an impossible task. It is hard on one who has undertaken to explain evolution in terms of the distribution of matter and motion to arrive at a stage where matter fails, and then to be compelled to deal with superorganic evolution. Hard, also, to have to speak of subject and object, and of other conceptions which decline to be subjected to a process of distribution and redistribution of matter and motion. We can but express our sympathy, and pass on to the conviction that the source of explanation lies not where they are seeking it. What has appeared in the process of evolution was there in the source from which evolution flowed. And what has appeared is a revelation of the living energy from which all things proceeded.

On this topic we quote from the Master of Balliol. "When, indeed, we turn back from the developed organism to the embryo, from the man to the child, we find that a study of the process of genesis casts no little light upon the nature of the being which is its result. The man becomes in a higher sense intelligible, when we trace him back to the child. But, primarily and in the first instance, it is the developed organism that explains the germ from which it grew, and without having seen the former we could have made nothing of the latter. No examination of the child could enable us to prophesy the man, if we had not previously had some experience of mature manhood; still less would an examination of the embryo reveal to us the distinct lineaments of the plant, or animal, or man. Nor would our insight be greatly helped by a knowledge of the environments in which the process of development was to take place.

"It is the full growth and expansion of this mighty tree, under whose shadow the generations of men have rested, that enables us to understand its obscure beginnings, when it was the least of all seeds. Development is not simply the recurrence of the same effects in similar circumstances, not simply the maintenance of an identity under a variation determined by external conditions. Hence it is impossible from the phenomena of one stage of the life of a developing being to derive laws which will adequately explain the whole course of its existence. The secret of the peculiar nature of such a being lies just in the way of regular transition in which, by constant interaction with external influences, it widens the compass of its life, unfolding continually new powers and capacities — powers and capacities latent in it from the first, but not capable of being foreseen with any definiteness by one who had seen only the beginning. It follows that, in the first instance at least, we must read development *backward* and not *forward*, we must find the key to the meaning of the first stage in the last, though it is quite true that, afterwards, we are enabled to throw new light upon the nature of the last, to analyze and appreciate it in a new way, by carrying it back to the first. We may derive an illustration of this characteristic of development from the idea of development itself; for the idea of development is one of the latest ideas whose meaning and value have been brought to light by the progress of man, and is itself the much wanted key to the history of that progress." ("The Evolution of Religion," Vol. I., pp. 44–8.)

To understand the processes of the world and the

light they cast on the ground and source of it, we must take our stand on the highest outcome of the life that is in the world. True, our highest explanation will not be ultimate, for the end is not yet, and our interpretation is available only for the stage at which we have arrived. A further manifestation will arrive by and by; meanwhile our appreciation may be true and valuable, so far as it goes.

H

IV

RATIONAL LIFE AND ITS IMPLICATIONS

FOLLOWING the line of development of life we come to a form which seems to sum up in itself all the characteristics of the lower forms, and to present to our view marks unknown before. At present we do not dwell on the line of descent, or of ascent from the first to the final form of living beings on the earth. We acknowledge that there are many links of connection between man and other forms of life. That has been made plain enough to all. On the physical side man is an animal, perhaps the highest and most complicated of all animal forms, but yet with evident marks of his relationship to them. Leaving the doctrine of descent untouched, for an inadequate treatment of it would serve no good purpose, and an adequate treatment of it, even if I had the requisite knowledge, would far exceed my limits, I remark that a determination of this question is not important for the aim I have in view. All that is necessary from the point of view of the doctrine of descent is, that we admit that in all physical respects man is closely related to other forms

of life. It is confessedly difficult to choose a form
from which man may be said to have been descended.
But physiologically and anatomically man is like all
the higher animals. No doubt there are differences,
but these are admitted even by those who advocate
the doctrine of descent. We pass on, therefore, to
another aspect of the subject.

Nor do I spend, at this stage, any time on the
views of Darwin and Romanes as to the relation
of animal to human intelligence. Much might be
said on this topic, and something may be said later.
What I am concerned with here is not how man
came to be, nor how physically he was evolved from
lower forms of life, nor how his intelligence is related to lower intelligences, but what can we discern
man to be physically, mentally, morally, and religiously now that he is here.

The first thing that we note about him is that he is
differently related to his environment from any other
living being. As far as mere organic equipment
is concerned, man is one of the most helpless of
animals. He is not so swift as some, nor so keen
of sight as others; his sense of smell, of sound, or of
touch is imperfectly developed in comparison with
the extraordinary development of the keenness of
the senses in some creatures. He has not teeth and
claws like the tiger, nor horns like a bull, nor can
he use his teeth for carpentering like the beaver.
There is scarcely a single physical quality in which

he is not surpassed by one or other of the lower forms of living creatures. Yet he has become master of them all. How? Well, first of all, he has found out a way of making his environment compensate for his organic defects. He has done this not as lower organizations do by organic modification, but by making instruments and tools to serve his purpose. That is the first note of man on which I lay stress. He makes tools. How much is implied in that fact I do not inquire at present, but it does mean something; at least there is a new departure. There is nothing of this kind to be met with among lower animals. Apes may fling stones or fruit at the passers-by, but no ape has ever set himself deliberately to fashion a tool to carry in his hand in readiness for the hour of need. The rudest tribes of which we have any knowledge have this power of making and using tools. In fact, we classify the ages of human development by reference to the tools they made and used. The first tools may have been those which lay ready to hand, as Tylor says, "Pebbles for slinging or hammering, sharp stone splinters to cut or scrape with, branches for clubs and spears, thorns or teeth to pierce with." ("Anthropology," p. 183.) In possession of tools and the power of making them he was furnished with the means of coping with animals far stronger than he.

In the first tool made, in the first instrument fashioned, there lay the possibility and the promise of all the vast instrumental command over nature characteristic of modern civilization. We do not need to dwell in detail on the development of this human art. It is a most interesting history, and much has been written on it. Men learned to make instruments of a more useful and powerful kind, they found more suitable and more ductile material for their instruments, they subjected the raw material they found in their environment to processes of manufacture, until they had bronze, and iron tools, and weapons. On the form of these weapons they also lavished their power of invention, so as to satisfy their sense of beauty as well as their desire to make the instruments effective. Tools, instruments for use, yes, and something more, — they discovered the use of fire. Very early in the history of man fire was discovered and pressed into their service. Having discovered fire they had a still more powerful means at their command. With it they had the power of modifying the climate in which they lived, and of modifying the products of nature into a form more fit for human use. Other results followed from this tool-making faculty. Clothing to protect them, houses to shelter them, and a thousand things, all of which formed new departures on the part of this, the latest form of life.

Clearly life has put itself to new uses, and taken on new qualities unknown in connection with lower forms of life. The relation to the environment is something new. Every change of life in response to the change of the environment has been organic. The only response living creatures could make was to put forth structures to provide for new needs. Feet were modified so that birds might swim, necks were elongated so that the creature might have a wider range from which to obtain food, and so on over the whole range of adaptation of living creatures to their environment. They could meet external changes only by corresponding changes of the organism. The expensiveness of organic change set an obvious limit on the possible advance of the living being. Up to the advent of man the condition of progress seemed to have been the possibility of organic change. With the advent of man the nature of progress seems to change.

Not that we are to regard man as altogether independent of his environment, nor are we to think of him as able to modify it so as to change it altogether. If we were to dream of such a possibility, the facts of the case would immediately refute our imagination; for gravitation works on us as on other organisms. Heat and cold affect us, and the seasons in their changes deal with us in their own way; our food and our drink must be taken in and assimilated, and, in short, our whole physical nature is in endless ways in relation to our environment. Nor is the influence limited to the daily and yearly changes that we experience in the slow succession of the ages. These changes accumulate, and thus man has been differentiated into the various races of mankind, with their characteristic marks and divisions. Differences of colour, stature, physical conformations of skull, skeleton, eyes, hair, and so on, appear as differences wrought in the various races of mankind, whose likeness to each other marks them as one. Man lives under conditions of time, space, climate, and a thousand other aspects of the environment, and he must respond to them all.

But the difference is that, while animals appear to respond to these conditions only in the way of organic modification, man responds to them in the way of organic modification, but also in another and an additional way. He adapts the environment to him by putting it to a use which he impresses on it—a use which was not there until he invented it. The stone which he chips until he can take a firm grasp of it means the appearance of a new quality of life, a new way of adaptation to the environment. On this we lay stress, as it is sufficient to give us a point of difference between man and other organisms, with regard to which there can be no difference of opinion. It is difficult to reach a satisfactory limit physically, intellectually, or psychologically at which we can say, here the difference between man and the lower animals begins to be manifest. Physically, there is a number of differences, but the correspondence between part and part throughout the organism of some animals and of man is so great that a satisfactory delimitation can scarcely be obtained. So, also, it may be said of the feelings, emotions, cognitions, that for every aspect of the mental nature of man, something resembling it may be forthcoming on an examination of mind in animals. So instead of taking our stand on these, with regard to which there might emerge endless argumentation, we simply mark this, on which there is no dispute, man is a tool-making animal. This one difference, rightly understood, gives in itself a number of other differences. It reveals the advent of a power which can use its environment in a new way for its own benefit. Looking at this from the point of view of advantage, the power of using instruments not organically related to the organism is of incalculable benefit in the struggle for existence. It gave the rational animal a superiority over those better equipped than himself in the race for life. Some creatures were swifter, some stronger, some better armed, some more cunning; but this new power enabled him to be, in effect, swifter, stronger, and wiser than all of them, and in large measure to press them into his service.

Stress is laid on this aspect, as it is a favourite way of stating the fact on the part of evolutionists. Reason did give the human species an advantage which grew from more to more. I do not protest, for it represents a truth. Intelligence is a weapon of enormous power, and the use of it has enthroned man as the most powerful of all creatures. Whether, regarded in this abstract way as only a weapon, it could have led on to the results we see, is another question. It is, of course, possible to look at reason only in this light, and to regard it as a cunning device fitted to give the possessor of it an advantage in the struggle for existence. It has been so regarded, and it has been insisted on by those who desire to explain human phenomena in terms of biology. Reason has been represented as if it acted only in the interests of the individual; but this topic we postpone for the moment, and shall return to it when we look at the theory of Mr. Benjamin Kidd.

Meanwhile let us follow for a little the significance of the change which has happened to living things by this new departure. Tools once made, and the power of making them once discovered, became one of the permanent gains of the race of men. Of this there was no reversal. More and better tools were made, better materials for the purpose were discovered, and tools might pass from hand to hand. It gave to man a new view of the uses to which he might put the environment, and he found that the environment lent itself readily to such uses. It led on to greater discoveries. With tools he could build a better and more commodious shelter from the extremes of heat and cold, could command a more steady supply of food, and a more convenient form of clothing. As he advanced in the application of his power to his environment, he found that it responded to his attempts, that it was not a fixed, unyielding thing with which he was in intercourse, but one that seemed elastic, accommodating, ready to take on the forms and adaptations which he desired. The earth would grow grain for him, would keep it for him, if he could persuade it to take the form of a storehouse, thus he could secure his food for a year or two before it was needed. Thus he caused his environment to meet his needs, to provide him with more ample accommodation, more and better food, warmth, when the natural source of warmth was obscured, clothing, when he lost the power of modifying himself to meet the varying seasons of the year, and so on. It is not necessary to add other particulars. We see the story.

We note that all this gain is at the expense of the environment. Gain made by life before the advent of man, was attained by the forthputting of more adapted structures on the part of the organism. Life advanced by modification of structure, and adaptation to a climate of large variation was conducted by changes of the organism, by growing a thicker coat of hair, and of a different colour, or by the use of many devices to which our attention is drawn by writers on natural history. All of them, however, were due to organic modification. But the rational being has ceased so far to modify himself, and modifies his environment instead. Clearly this is a significant change, and one which gives us a new conception of the significance of life and its possibilities.

Then we pass on to ask how this gain is to be conserved, and how it is to be handed on to the succeeding generations of the human race. Up to this time the gain made by one generation or one individual animal could be handed on only to his own posterity, that is, if we suppose that acquired qualities can be transmitted. The line of transmission of acquired qualities could only be the line of descent. This was, however, a hazardous line of action. For accidents might happen to the strongest, most highly evolved, individual of the species; and his qualities could not be transmitted if he had no offspring. Organic modification was clearly an unsatisfactory means either for the acquisition or the transmission of the gains won by the species in the race for good. One might predict that the rational being who had found a way, or for whom a way had been found, of making an advance without modifying himself, would also find a way by which the gain would be preserved.

Here there comes to our view the first sign of the truth that reason is not a disintegrating, disuniting power, but a power which makes for unity, progress, and integration. To preserve and increase the gain won by him who had made the first tool, there was needed a way by which that power could be communicated to others not necessarily in the line of direct descent. Reason found a way, a way unknown before. Whatever may be the extent of communication between animal and animal, it is evident that that way is not to be compared with the way in which man may communicate with man. The instrument which man has found for the conservation of his hard won gain is language, which, when once won, increased the practical power of reason immeasurably. It preserved the past, it led on to greater gain in the future.

Now this instrument which is the offspring of reason, which reflects and embodies reason, is manifestly a social product. The very rudiments of speech indicate the fact that it arose because men had learned to work together. To be able to name a thing so that others might recognize it by the name, to have a cry which would indicate the approach of anger, to have a word the speaking of which would give a signal for a pull altogether, the power to communicate to his fellow what was in his own mind, and all the other facilities so well known to us that we seldom think of them, are of immense significance as we look at them when they were a new thing in the manifestation of life. It is another illustration of the fact that man advances by modifying his environment. The tongue and ear, in the service of reason, use the atmosphere for their own intelligent purposes. First for communication to one another of their thoughts, wishes, desires, and then for the conservation of their gains. Manifestly the power gained by men was vastly increased by the discovery of this new instrument. Words spoken could be remembered, the experience of one could be communicated to another by the use of this instrument, and a youth could set out on the warpath instructed by the warning of those who had had experience of war.

The lessons of experience could be handed on to others. What men had learned of land and sea, of wood and river, of the nature, habits, and mode of life of the animals they followed in the chase, might be told, and the gain could be conserved and handed on merely by the use of speech and not by hereditary transmission alone. So far as we have come we find that the advent of reason means deliverance from the control of mere biological processes. The making of tools was the discovery of a less costly way of adaptation to the environment than that which life had heretofore followed. The discovery of the power of speech was the establishment of a means of maintaining and extending the gains of men beyond the means of transmission by descent, apparently the only means of transmitting gain which life had formerly discovered. We shall have many other illustrations of this as we proceed.   At present we lay stress on these two, as in themselves a sufficient proof that biology is helpless in the presence of these new phenomena.   The processes described by biology, as adequate for all beings up to man, are clearly inadequate here.   It is not possible to deal with man as a mere biological animal.

Nor is it possible to deal with man as if he were a mere individual.   Looking back to the advent of speech, we see that the very condition of its advent was that man was a social being.   Obviously speech implies men living together, conscious of common needs, of common aims, and of common powers requiring expression.   A solitary individual would neither feel the need nor have the power of speech. But a solitary individual need not be considered, as he is only the abstract possibility which exists simply for the purpose of making a certain philosophy conceivable.   What that philosophy is we shall see by and by.   Meanwhile we may take it as axiomatic that language is a social product.   Its existence is a proof that the individual exists as a rational human being in relation to society, that he can be, grow, develop his rational powers, only in intercourse with his fellows.

Tool-making and speech introduce us to such modifications of the environment as make it largely new.   If we are to understand the progress of man, we must look at him not as if he were in intercourse

with an environment which is fixed and unchangeable, but with one which changes from age to age
by those modifications which are due to the rational
being himself. A world modified by the instruments
made by man is a different world from what it was
before the advent of that advance. At all events
it is different to man. A larger difference appears
when man discovered the way to speak. Now the
environment is not the old environment which sur-
rounded men before speech was discovered; it is the
old, plus the change wrought for him by the presence
of human beings who can speak and tell him of their
experience. The environment is no abstraction; it is
a real concrete thing of amazing complexity, a complexity that varies to every individual. We are apt
to place an abstract individual in an abstract environment, but that is not the way of reality. The
environment of the rational being who had advanced
so far as to make tools and to speak had taken on
new meanings, and every rational being born into it
had an environment enriched by all the experience of
the race. Not wind and weather, sun, moon, or stars,
not all the physical surroundings of his existence,
made up his environment, but to these were added
the care of parents during his prolonged infancy and
his helpless childhood, the training he received, the
beliefs he saw in his acquaintances, and the thousand
influences which moulded him. This was the environment of the rational being.

Again, we say we must widen our biological method if we are to understand the nature of a rational being. To speak of environment in the large and general way now fashionable, is to mislead. The environment is relative to the organism, as the organism is relative to the environment. A dog seems to live in a world of smells, and other animals in a world suited to their prevailing characteristics. A thousand kinds may live in a square mile of ground, and each of them may have a different environment. An organism so far selects its own environment, and takes from it what it needs. It is time to put something like an arrest on the attempt to apply to the rational being those methods of interpretation which may have been found adequate in a lower sphere, but when applied here can only mislead. Man's environment is largely made by man.

As we follow on down the stream of time we see this rational being making more advances. We do not see that advance is always made, or that reason always hits the mark. On the contrary, we see enough of mistakes, many blunders, much stumbling, as it tries unaccustomed ways. Reason has had sometimes to pay a price for the advantages it has won for man. The tentative blundering way in which it reaches forth after the accomplishment of its aims, the way it uses inadequate means for its ends, the miscalculations and failures it makes, are in striking contrast to the sureness, accuracy, and completeness with which other animals achieve their more limited results. It takes time for reason to find out what means will achieve certain ends. Trial after trial is made, failure is added to failure, but reason has the power of learning from its failures, and of making them stepping-stones to higher things.

Nor is the heritage which rational men have handed on to their successors always a heritage of goodness, or righteousness, or truth. It is no story of unmingled good nor of untroubled progress that history has to tell regarding the human race. From one point of view the story of life may be told as a story of progress, if we neglect the failures and have regard only to those who have succeeded. But not even this can be said of the human story. The advent of reason, if in one way a signal advance, is in another way a story of retrogression. True, it won for man the mastery over other races, but it did not enable him to master himself. Powerful to enable him to adapt himself to his environment, and his environment to him, it seemed powerless to guide him on to truth, goodness, and love. As we look at reason at work, in the earlier races of men, it seems to be in the service of every lust and every passion that rise within the heart or lure the mind on to the gratification of the baser feelings and desires. Reason does not seem to be even coördinated with the desires and passions, it seems to be a servant to them. It is far from having attained the supremacy which it apparently ought to have. The advent of reason, from an ethical point of view, results in a degradation and a fall. In some ways it brought man below the level of the higher animals. Lust, desire, passion, in a rational being, took a deeper and a more malignant form. Reason enabled the rational being to picture the object of desire in more alluring forms, and put something like an infinite element into it.

The lusts and desires of other animals were excited only while the objects of them were within their reach; but the rational being could treasure them up in memory, paint them in imagination, linger over them in anticipation and in retrospect, until he ordered his reason to use all means for the gratification of his desire. Passions and desires partake of the higher nature of reason. They may be transformed from their original teleological function, and the gratification of them may and sometimes does become an end in itself. With the higher animals, feelings, passions, desires, seem to be always teleological; they are for the furtherance of the good of the individual and of the race. When the teleological end is reached, the animal seems satisfied. With the rude human being the mere teleological reference seems to become confused, uncertain; as if reason had paralyzed instinct, and the gratification of the lust of the moment had become an end in itself. How shall the human being learn self-knowledge, self-reverence, self-control? It is the problem of destiny for the human being. For other animals had a guide for conduct; they were under the imperious dictation of instinct, that proceeded to its end with a precision that seemed infallible. Their ideal was easily realized, if it can be called an ideal. But for the rational being the advent of reason seemed to have set him free from the sure guidance of teleological function, and to have cast him loose on a sea of adventure. Reason had at once raised him higher and sunk him lower than the other animals.

Thus we see him set out on his perilous path, slowly trying to feel his way to the recognition of a standard of conduct, and to substitute rational self-guidance for the leading of instinct. It would be long to tell the story of his failures and success; and in what I do say, I wish not to go beyond the domain of science. It is a pathetic story that science tells us of the efforts of the earliest men in their search after a standard of conduct. The story is often told in an unfriendly, unsympathetic way, as if science rejoiced to show us how rude and lowly were the beginnings of our science, our ethics, our philosophy, and our religion. True, their beginnings were lowly and rude enough, but still a beginning was made. There is something to me very great in the first sign of recognition by man of a rule of conduct, other than the gratification of his own desires. Science may tell me truly that the taboo, or the command which prohibited a certain course of conduct, was superstitiously believed and observed, and I shall say nothing to the contrary; but I do say that the recognition by man of something sacred, of something which he must not touch or desire, of commands which he must unconditionally obey, was a great step on the way by which he might learn that for him there was a rational ideal which he was bound to realize. As yet he had nothing worthy of the great names of science, philosophy, ethics, or religion. He is simply a rational being, whose rationality has not realized itself.

With rationality exercised in the way of making tools and employed in speech, some restraints on the lawlessness of human desires must speedily have arisen. Habits were formed, actions were discovered to be harmful to one's self and injurious to others, and these were prohibited. As experience widened, the number of these grew until there would exist something like a code for conduct. At present I am not dealing with supernatural sanctions for conduct, though almost all actions were regarded by primitive man as subject to, and prescribed by, a supernatural power. Leaving that fact alone for the present, let us follow on along the line I have indicated.

How is reason to act in harmony with all the other faculties of man? In other words, how shall man become altogether rational? How shall reason enter into and transform the emotions, cognitions, and volitions of man, until they become the feelings, thoughts, and actions of a rational, self-guided being? For reason is used by me in that wide sense, and the goal of a rational being is that he is to become rational all through. As we read the story of a man pictured to us by the students of anthropology, we see him in a very rude and uncultured state. He has tools, fires, shelter, food; he has speech, as the earliest records of him abundantly show. He has subdued certain other animals and pressed them into his service. He has certain thoughts about the world in which he is, but it is largely a world not realized. He has not reached the thought of a fixed order of the world; forms of life and death have given to him certain thoughts about them, and about himself. He has learned that certain actions he must not do, certain things he must not touch, and certain ceremonies he must perform. He believes that if he transgress the one or omit the doing of the other, he will pay the penalty. Habits become fixed, beliefs grow, and a standard of conduct emerges, and these develop into institutions, which again have a reflex influence on those who live under them. These are realities for those who are born and grow up under their influence. They are part of their environment.

A little later we find that man has formed for himself a rule of conduct, consisting of rules of a very drastic kind. The individual is almost lost to sight, and what we find is a company of men the actions and relations of which are prescribed, and whose very thoughts are bound into a system of rules. The unit seems to be, not the individual, but the family or the tribe, and the individual has no rights and no freedom; he is merely a member of the tribe. As soon as organization appeared it seems to have been carried to an extreme. The existing savage and the rude man of primitive times are bound together in the most rigid fashion by a set of most elaborate rules, all of which are enforced by the most awful sanctions. Whatever may be the origin of these rules which bind the mind and guide the action of the ruder tribes of men, there can be no doubt of their existence. The evidence is abundant and clear. Rules regarding his relation to the world of objects around him, rules regarding his relations to the other members of the tribe, rules concerning marriage, rules regarding his attitude toward the unseen powers on which he felt his dependency, were ever present and operative on him.

Thus a check on the lawlessness of the individual was obtained, but apparently at a high price. The individual was sacrificed to the society, and the good of the tribe seemed to be the end of these elaborate rules. At all events, whether that was what was meant, that was accomplished. Among the rudest tribes and in the beginnings of civilization, what we find is not the individual, but the clan or tribe. Power is in the hands of the father or the mother, in the hands of the chief or the priest, and every rule served to add to the further consolidation of that power. This was one way of harnessing reason and of making it work within bounds and on certain lines. Having dislocated the action of instinct, and having introduced uncertainty where certainty obtained in lower animals, reason was uneasy until it obtained another kind of instinct, one instituted, guided, and made by itself. For the characteristic of reason is that it must justify to itself the action it prescribes. It must give a reason for its action. Whether it was a true or adequate reason is another question.

Customs, habits, beliefs, arose among men and grew into a system, a system which has varied in content and form with the different races of men. One thing we observe with regard to them all is that each had its explanation of the origin, meaning, and sanction of their rites and customs. Having obtained the rule and acted on it, having established the custom and made it binding, the rational being set himself to find reasons for his practice. What he set forth as explanation is to be found in the mythologies of the race. Mythology is largely explanation. It is the science, the philosophy, the theology, of the races of men. As we read these mythologies, — and nowadays they take much time to read them, —

we greatly admire the ingenuity and versatility of our ancestors. They were not content with mere acceptance of the customs, rites, ordinances, which were handed down to them, and made binding on them; they endeavoured to make their assent to their observance rational. The explanation found was such as was possible to a rational being whose rationality was not yet consciously realized by himself. But the main thing to observe is that an explanation was felt to be needed; the kind of explanation that was forthcoming is not so important for our purpose.

It is another element in the system of differences between the being who is at least implicitly rational, and the animal that remains irrational to the end, that the one seeks for an explanation of his experience and the other does not. The primitive man asked himself and others regarding the origin of things, their meaning, their ongoing, their goal; he asked also about himself, and his relations to what was beneath, around, and above him. His answers to these questions are to be found in the mythologies and religions which are so sympathetically studied to-day. We have our theories of mythology, we speak of animism, of the worship of ancestors, of polytheism, of theism, and of the strange experience of the human race, and of the explanation of their experience which they set forth for themselves. Sometimes our theories are a bed of Procrustes for the poor facts, which are mangled and tortured in the process. Happily the facts survive, and their sufficient explanation will be reached by and by.

Meanwhile let us say that in these mythologies of the past we have the rudiments of the science of to-day. Here is man's first recorded recognition of the uniformities of nature. That water would assuage thirst to-day and to-morrow, that fruits would satisfy hunger, that the animals he chased and caught to-day indicated that animals of the same kind would behave in a similar way when he followed again in pursuit, that the sun would continue to rise and give him light and heat, and that there was a time for the growing and ripening of things and for their decay, would soon be borne in upon his mind, and serve to regulate his conduct. Other uniformities would be added as experience widened, likely. The fact that things maintained their properties from day to day must have been soon learned by him. Likeness and unlikeness impressed the primitive man as they impress his descendants, and a rude classification of them would be formed. So science began to be, not in its separateness as with us, but mixed up with many explanations which were not scientific.

But the unscientific explanation of the primitive man does not affect the fact that here were the beginnings of science, or the truth of the science which

has grown from such a beginning.   Science of a kind
is there, even if it be only in the form of a recognition of a permanence in things and their behaviour.
Is it contended that early man looked at all things
from his own standpoint and thought that everything
had a spirit and life in it?   Is animism the science
of the primitive man?   It is so said by Dr. Tylor.
I have some doubts as to whether there is evidence
to warrant such a conclusion.   That man could not
distinguish between the living and the non-living
seems to me an incredible proposition.   That he
thought some non-living things to have a kind of
life seems to be true, but he had some special reason
for that belief.   Mr. Spencer explains the matter by
the supposition that the primitive man thought a
ghost had taken possession of the non-living object,
and he therefore accepted it as living.   It is allowable to accept Mr. Spencer's testimony that there
is a fact to be explained, though we cannot accept
his explanation.   But the question is too large for
discussion here.

What I am concerned with is the fact that science
began as soon as man recognized the uniformity of
nature in some things at least.   That these uniformities were recognized is apparent from the mythologies themselves.   Still further, these mythologies
furnish us with the rudiments of a philosophy and
an ethic.   They contain the first reflections of men
on the beginnings of things, and on the causes

which produced them. Very childish and very pathetic they seem to us as we read of the rise of the world and the making of man, but we again say that they form a tribute to the greatness of man. To ask the question, even though they could find no answer, shows that life had put forth new phenomena. If early man found an explanation of the universe in chaos, and dwelt on a way in which chaos did come to an ordered world, well! modern philosophy, in some moods and in some minds, does go back to a lifeless chaotic cloud of fifty million years ago. Others again dwell on the persistence of force, and tell of a wonderful transformation by which the homogeneous becomes heterogeneous. It would appear that with regard to origins we are as helpless as they.

To mythology as bearing on theology and religion, we shall return at a later stage of our argument. For the right understanding of the philosophy and ethics of early man, we have to look at the institutions which he has formed. The fundamental institution is the family. It was a long time in the history of man before the family was recognized in its ethical significance. The history of marriage is a sad story, and the whole business can scarcely be described. The relations between the sexes were no doubt subject to certain regulations even in the rudest tribes, and a restraint of some kind was laid on the lusts of man. But it is evident that until monogamous marriage became the rule, ethical progress could scarcely be attained. This lies at the foundation of family life; and the moral state of a community may be estimated by the regard they have to the holiness of family life. For the family is the first and most important of those institutions which help to mould the opening life of a young man or woman. The unsatisfactory character of man's ethical development may be largely traced to the fact that the ideal of a family appears comparatively late in the history. Instead of a family in the proper sense of the word, we may have a matriarchate in which kinship was reckoned by the mother, or a polygamous establishment in which the relation of parent and child had little ethical significance, or there may be polyandry; in fact, you may have and actually have all kinds of relationships established between men and women into which purity, permanence, and equality did not enter. Still into such imperfect relationships there entered something of the tender self-sacrifice of a mother's love, and something of a father's providing care. The helplessness of a child during its prolonged infancy made a strong appeal to the mother, and drew forth something of love, of exquisite tenderness, and devoted service.

Thus, while the ideal of a real family lay in the distant future, and could not be realized until reason had come to a larger fulfilment, enough was attained to show forth what a family ideal might come to be, when human character would attain to a more rational completeness.   As it was in the olden world, marriage could not attain its ideal end.   It was too often the source of contradiction and confusion, and both the physiological fact of sex and the emotional fact of sexual love became antagonistic to the very notion of ethics.   They were too often separated from their teleological function, and men were powerless to transfigure them into that higher order in which the light of reason works through love. Still, even in their imperfection, they enable us to see in the mutual love of parents and children, in the mutual bonds that made the family one, and in the service of self-sacrifice which the members of a family felt bound to render to one another, the promise of a larger future.   In the family the first lessons of experience are learned, the discovery is made that the child is one among others, bound up with others in a larger unity, and held together with them in the bonds of common interests and common work.   Such lessons as these could be learned in the imperfect family of the ancient world.   Further, the children of the house had at their disposal all the experience of the parents.   In the family they learned to speak, to name things and to use them, they learned to love and to work.   On the other hand, parents simply as parents rose to a greater height as human beings, their hearts throbbed with a greater love, they looked at life with a wider outlook, and they rose in the scale of being, because of the young beings whose life was bound up in theirs.

In the family life, even of the olden world, we find the great sphere of ethical training. Here is the first lesson that reason learned in its endeavour to make for itself a rational world. Here an individual predisposed to use reason for himself alone as a mere instrument for his own pleasure, or glory, learned that reason had a grander meaning and a wider purpose. The individual learned that he was not separate and isolated, that in fact he could only find himself by losing himself, and find himself transformed and glorified by knowing himself (as Hegel has said) as the unity of himself with another and of another with him. Such is the love that lies at the basis of family life. Then comes the larger life of the family, when fathers and mothers find themselves in the unity which is made up of parents and children. Glorified in fatherhood and motherhood as children are given to them, glorified still further as the children win more room in their hearts, parents give more and more love as they watch the growing intelligence, the warm affection, and the thousand winning ways of children. This is the first school of humanity, good for the lessons taught to parents and to children. Here we learn the first lessons in self-reverence, self-knowledge, self-control. Here we find the first example of the great ethical law that a man must lose himself in order to find himself.

Speaking for myself, I must say that I feel unspeakably grateful to Hegel and to the many eminent men who work in philosophy under the inspiration and the hope inspired by Hegel, for the wondrous light they have cast on the significance of the family. I say this all the more emphatically as I do not agree with them in some of their contentions. "The unity which is founded on natural feeling," says Professor Mackenzie, "must precede that which depends on acquired sympathies and thoughts. To begin with the love of humanity, would be to begin with a cold abstraction. The family is like a burning glass, which concentrates human sympathies on a point. Within that narrow circle selfishness is gradually overcome, and wider interests developed. Each one is supplied with the opportunity of knowing a few human beings thoroughly, than which nothing is more important as a first stage in the transcendence of the merely individual self. One who knows only himself inwardly, and sees others only by a kind of outward observation, which in a large circle is an almost inevitable result, is apt to become for himself too entirely the centre of his world, if, indeed, he ever forms a world or cosmos for himself at all. The family enables a few persons to become not merely objects for each other, but parts of a single life; and the unity thus effected may then be very readily extended as sympathies grow." ("Social Philosophy," pp. 363-4, 2d edition.)

Parts of a single life — it is a significant phrase, and states in few words the ethical significance of the family when it is properly constituted. But it presupposes that the family proceeds from one union and not from many, from one centre formed by two who have found themselves in each other. But we shall not return to the undeveloped family life of the early races of mankind. On that, enough has been said already. We may reassert, however, that imperfect though it was, it yet had an important bearing on the training of men, and it helped them to know that reason was not theirs in order to be used as an instrument for the gaining of merely individual ends, but that it was theirs in order that man might recognize himself as a part of a whole, and that he could not realize himself save in relation to a whole. This has an unspeakable significance for the development of man, as a sane and sound, moral and rational, being. We have laid stress on the family as the sphere in which this has been effectively done. The unity of the family is a moral and spiritual unity, constituted by spiritual bonds. The unity of an organism is physical and visible, and is constituted for organic ends. It is one of the functions of reason to transcend the unities constituted by organic ends, and to recognize larger unities, based on bonds which do not reveal themselves to sense, and cannot be traced by physical causation. The bond which holds the family together is moral and spiritual, and is cognizable only by a rational being, as it can be constituted by rational beings alone. The beginning of such a possibility is to be thankfully recognized, and the growth of it is one of the signs which herald the coming of a better day for humanity. It was a great triumph when the rational being recognized himself as a member of a larger whole, and comprehended that bonds which he could not touch, nor see, nor handle, were stronger, and held him with a firmer grasp than any physical bond could do. There were many agencies needed to bring about this great end. And of these agencies the family was the first and one of the strongest. But then the family was only after all one circle within a larger circle, and the life which had no interest beyond the family was a contracted life. It might look at reason as an instrument to be used only for the advance of the family, and the struggle of reason against selfishness might be repeated in this larger sphere. The completeness of the family and the satisfaction which the members found in one another might hinder them from the recognition that the family could find their ethical significance only in the recognition of the fact that they were members of a still larger whole. Thus on every step of the upward spiral, the conflict between the selfish and

the rational was renewed. It still goes on and will
go on, until the worth and freedom of the individual
are recognized, and the fact accepted that the worth
and value of the individual can only be realized in
a society which receives his all from him and returns
it to him enhanced a thousand fold.

V

THE MAKING OF MAN

SOMETHING of the significance of the family has been seen; and the part it plays in the evolution of man is great. Part of the heritage of humanity belongs to the parents before they have come together; stores of spiritual energy laid up for them in the tradition of the ages. But it is in the faces of the father and the mother that the child finds, in concrete form, the touch that wakens up the dull materials of humanity and quickens them into emotional and spiritual life. Spiritual parentship takes the place of merely natural parentship, and in the interchange of affection between parents and children, fatherhood and sonship take on an added glory. The child reveals to the parents depths of life undreamed of before; gives a new centre to existence, a new stimulus to effort, and builds for them a wider horizon and a larger future.

As has been said already, the family is only one stage of the progress of man. Beyond the family is dimly seen the wider circle of the tribe, and the city. We say dimly seen, for in the early ages the vision is not distinct. The gain was very slow, and not for a long time have we the emergence of the state. True, we have at an early stage in history gigantic specimens of world empires, in which the few seemed to use the many for their own purposes, simply as instruments. The ancient world empire was no realized ideal of happiness or progress for men. True, the works remain to this hour; symbols of many things, and are fitted to give rise to many reflections. We wonder at the skill, labour, coöperation, and resources of the generations that built the pyramids, and baked the bricks of Babylon. But these — triumphs of organization though they were — did not give the promise of permanence, for the organization was impressed on the individuals from above and from without, and did not guarantee a corresponding inward growth of the individual. The building of world empires was premature, and they passed away.

All along the line of progress we see the conflict between the individual and what we may call society. The individual tends in irrational fashion to look at reason and all its implications as something to be used for himself, irrespective of the claims of others. While association in family life gives him some idea of the obligation that lies on him to regard the claims of others, speedily the family becomes simply a larger unity, the interests of which may be regarded as in conflict with the interests of others. Rivalry, competition, and conflict are renewed on the larger scale, and the family is held in abstraction precisely as the individual was held in abstraction and looked at as a separate being bound up in his own interests. Similarly, the tribe became a unit of abstraction, and its interests were held to be in conflict with the interests of others. Thus the course of history is marked by conflicts of all kinds, and conflicts which assumed a larger scale as the organized unities of men became larger and larger. Wars between individuals became the vendettas of families; these became wars between villages, and these in turn became the strife between states, and the struggle continued on a larger scale, and it is not over yet.

The conflict was not altogether evil. There were many features of the human character which could be developed only through conflict. Courage, endurance, skill, foresight, command of oneself and of the resources of life, might be developed through the call which war made on the faculty of man. Nor were these all. The other-regarding virtues, also, found opportunity of realization. Loyalty to leaders, obedience, trust, self-sacrifice, and a passion for the country which gave a man birth, grew in the conflict. The effect produced on the mind of a people by a continued conflict with their neighbours may be the production of the other-regarding disposition. Much might be written from this point of view, and a great deal of what is good and worthy has been written. What a wealth of inspiring thought and high-souled emotion lies in the war songs of a people! The iron hand of war gripped them, welded them into a unity, made them feel the pulse of a common life, made them quiver at the thought of a common danger, made them feel vividly, as they would not otherwise have felt, the unity of a mother country, as if she were their mother indeed, and reinforced the feeling of patriotism with a thousand associations in which there was nothing mean or sordid. Patriotism aroused somehow, stimulated and quickened by all the associations of dangers manfully faced and overcome, of triumphs won by bravery, courage, and endurance, forms one of the stages in the upward progress of humanity.

A flood of war to rebaptize the nations; yes, war has had that effect once and again in the history of the world. The trials and triumphs of war have had their permanent effects on human character and development. If we limit our view to one people, and refuse to look across the border, we might speak at length on the development of the manly virtues, might sing that it is sweet to die for one's native country, and dwell on the reflex results on human character, and the widening of the bounds of feeling, and so on. In the same way we might dwell on the struggle for existence in the lower world, and show eloquently how the strong became stronger, and the swift, swifter, until the higher races appeared. In neither the one case nor the other is the picture an alluring one. In both cases, I must say, that as I read, I long for a heaven for the failures, for some compensation for the unsuccessful. And verily they have had their compensation, and the meek inherit the earth. But of this I shall speak later on.

The story of this incessant competition may be read from another point of view. I read it not so much in relation to the victory which one people, city, or tribe wins over another, as in the light which it casts on the growth of human character. It is a step in the process of welding men together, it is one of the cases in which something produces its opposite. The war, which had such sad results when looked at from one point of view, had good effects on the nation who made war. It taught the rational being that he had wider interests than his personal interests, that he had larger aspirations than those of his family or his tribe, and it taught him that all his rational powers ought to be used in the service of the wider unity. The devotion of a man to the state, the development of the thought of duty to the fatherland, the discovery of himself as a citizen of the state, as a responsible member of a larger whole, was a great gain, won, as all ethical gains are won, at a tremendous cost.

The cost is great, and grows in magnitude as one thinks of it. Strife everywhere, man against man, tribe against tribe, city against city, state against state, reason turned from its ideal and made an instrument of disintegration, is that the record of history, and the condition of progress? Are men to grow into larger and larger unities, to organize themselves into wider communities, in order to coöperate for war on a larger scale? Every stranger an enemy, and every one of unknown speech one to be attacked, such appeared to be the state of the human race at one time, and it is not unusual to-day. The problem is to think out how this process will result in our higher civilization, with its ethics, philosophy, religion, with its sense of the value of the individual, and of the worth of human life. It is a great and difficult problem, look at it as we may.

A problem less difficult may occupy us first. How shall there be brought into existence a visible community of men and women united together in such a way that there will result a coördination and subordination of individuals and their actions toward some common end that belongs to all, and can be enjoyed by each? The first solution of the problem is the family. There it has found a partial solution, but only on a small scale, and for a short time. The unity, observe, is not merely organic; if it is to exist at all, it must be constituted out of elements so far independent of each other as to be individuals who can move, act, think, feel, and will on their own account. In other words, the unity must be constituted on rational grounds and upheld by rational beings, who have the power of disrupting at their pleasure. I am aware that the social contract no longer appears in philosophy, and aware, also, that constitutions grow and are not manufactured. I have put the matter as I did merely for the sake of stating the problem, and of enabling us to realize what a problem it is. Carlyle puts a parallel problem, "Given a world of knaves, to deduce an honesty from their united action." Given a world of apparently disunited beings, how will you train them to act together, to care for a common interest, and to recognize that they must work together, if they are to obtain a good worth having? As I said, the first answer is the family. In it a common interest is obvious, and feeling and affection help to build up this unity of love and mutual benefit.

Beyond the family there are again obvious common ways of action, and bonds of union. Trade, commerce, union for a temporary purpose, which requires coöperation and mutual trust for its realization, these readily occur to us all. Outside of particular families, and yet within the larger unity of the state, people unite themselves in a thousand ways for different ends, drawn together because they form friendships with each other, or united because they follow a common pursuit. These bonds are voluntarily constituted, and are all the stronger and more disinterested on that account. Within the larger society there may be many people associated together for special ends, and the educative power of such unions may be great. In these the compulsory character of merely natural unions slips into the background, and men learn that though they have formed bonds for themselves, they are not less bound, but more. Along the line of such association freely formed, and carried out with honour and fidelity, is to be found a large part of the moral education of mankind. For the need is to prevent the gift of reason from being merely the addition of a disruptive element to life.

That such a view of the quality which distinguishes man from other animals may be taken is quite apparent. It has been taken by the possessors themselves, and, also, by those who have speculated on the question. By the possessors themselves, for, as we have seen, it is one of the hardest problems that have emerged in history to persuade men that a selfish use of reason is irrational. It seems almost to be a law of history that only one good result can be won at one time. Human growth seems to be made by the process of laying emphasis on one thing at a time, to the neglect of another which in the long run is of equal importance. It would almost seem that in order that a truth may be recognized at all, it must be emphasized as if it were the whole truth. The immediate illustration of this law is that of the relation of the individual to society. In order that the individual may learn to know that he is little in himself, apart from his fellows, the way of his training, as we see it in history, is to bind him with his fellows in so drastic a fashion that he is scarcely able to make any movement on his own account.

Rules gird him about, customs cluster around him, his feeling, thought, action, are prescribed for him, and apparently for him there is no initiative, and scarcely any independent course. Actions are done because others have done them, observances are held because they have been handed down, and in all the round of the experience of every day the course is prescribed. Certain trades are hereditary; men are bound to live and work as their fathers did; castes are formed; in fact, illustrations of this are so numerous that it is not needful to enter into detail. Formed as they were in the early ages of the human race, they must from the nature of the case be rude, irrational, and inadequate. But it may have been the only way of teaching the rational being the necessity of recognizing the wider claims of reason. As obedience was the way of fitting a man for the responsibility of command, so the way of teaching the individual the responsibility attached to rationality as such, was to bind him in bonds which almost rendered disobedience impossible. At all events that has been the historical method of training the rational being and of teaching him the right use of reason.

As at one time the making of rules for the guidance of man seemed to be the main object of society, there came a time when the breaking of rules, shown to be inadequate, and the criticism of beliefs proven to be without evidence, came to be the highest duty of man. The making of rules, as well as the breaking of them, was alike the work of the rational being. Late in human history came the recognition of the fact that rules were made for man, not man for rules. To put it more clearly, the discovery of the individual person and his worth appears as one of the latest achievements of man. We might write a philosophy of history from this point of view. We might set forth the strenuous work of the earliest races of the human family to subdue the merely selfish rational being and make him subject to the dominating claims of the whole. The success of that task might seem to be almost too complete. Then there might be set forth the slow process of the emancipation of the individual from the chains and shackles forged for him by the rules, traditions, and customs of society.

How many mighty movements of the historic ages converge toward this end! For us modern men the mightiest are Rome, Greece, and Palestine. The great structure of Roman law is one of the mightiest achievements of the human mind. Its vast and majestic form stands at the beginning of our modern civilization, and, in its completeness, it sets forth and vindicates the mutual coördination of all in the one great system in which both gods and men had their place and their part. Each person had his position and his rights, and these could be vindicated if any one encroached on them. Much might be said on this were there time. Alongside of the debt we owe to Rome is the debt we owe to Greece. The philosophy of Greece, its reflection on nature, on art, on the city-state, on man as a thinker, on man as an individual, as a member of the state, as a being free and yet under law; in fact, all the mighty achievements of Greece in science and philosophy were elements for the solution of the great problem of the relation of man to men and of men to man. But not from Rome nor from Greece did the greatest service come toward the recognition of the worth of the individual. To another people much is due, and from another source did the greatest influence toward the emancipation of the individual from the irrational bonds that bound him come. From the Hebrews, too, came the recognition of the immense worth of the individual life and of the contribution which the individual might make to the worth of humanity. It was from the Hebrews that the largest contribution came, the worth of which we shall not attempt now to measure. From Rome, Greece, and Palestine came those mighty influences that moulded man, and fitted him to ask the question of how society is to be built up, without the sacrifice of the individuality of the individual. Notwithstanding the mighty influences of these historic peoples, and notwithstanding the new spirit that breathed over man at the advent of Christianity, it was a long time before men consciously faced the question,—of the relation of man to men. When it was raised by Descartes in his own way, and when he asked for a rational sanction for everything that he could question, he opened the way for a reaction that isolated the individual, insisted on his independent worth, and actually left the notion of society out of account. It was a time great in abstractions: an abstract mind was beside an abstract body, and men made for themselves the great problem of getting body and mind again in relation. It was a time, too, when men looked at everything as fixed, static, unchangeably determined in its own nature, and the problem is like the problem of biology to-day,—how to get the organism back into unity after they have disrupted it into fragments.

So, also, with regard to the relation of the individual to society, men had to invent ways of restoring the lost unity. The abstract individual restored to some recognition of his relative independence, had his revenge on the society which had enslaved him. So, too, the abstract individual set his discoverers to a task harder than ever was Egyptian bondage. Given the abstract individual in his completeness and independence, to construct society, that was the problem of a philosophy which started from the individual. It would be long to tell the story of the social contracts, of the liberty, equality, and fraternity; of the devices which were set forth as the way in which society was constituted out of independent individuals. It was a reaction against that method which neglected the individual, which made him merely a link in a chain, and gave him no position of worth in relation to society. But like all reactions it went too far. It in its turn neglected the other factor.

The literature of the Aufklärung is instructive in many ways. Nor are we done with it yet. It is with us to-day on our side of the water, and, perhaps, on your side too. From it, in particular, we have got those definitions of reason and rationalism which have made it seem to be the private property of the individual, which has set it in opposition to other parts of human nature, and given occasion to the contrarieties of reason and faith, reason and authority, and of other contradictions within human nature, which have played a great part in modern thought. Of course, if you begin with the individual, whether it be an individual atom, or anything else, you can scarcely persuade the individual to become part of a system. It is easy to take a watch to pieces, it takes a skilled workman to put it together again. Starting as it did from the individual, laying stress on his separateness and isolation as it did, the philosophy of individualism had to fall back on artificial ways in order to restore somehow the social unity which it had disrupted. It was the counterpart of the previous age-long movement that had resulted in the suppression of the individual. It did a good work for human thought in laying emphasis on the neglected factor. It taught us that if we are to understand ourselves and our cosmical position, we must travel from society to the individual, and from the individual to society, and not till we have done both shall we be prepared to make that synthesis which shall recognize that each is for the other, in the other, and that taken apart they fall into meaninglessness.

Leaving for subsequent treatment the conception of personality, let us set ourselves to think of the largest unity we have yet reached. Humanity is one, subsisting in real connection of whole and part from the first appearance of man until the present day; all the generations are linked together in unbroken sequence, and each generation adds to the tradition of its predecessors; it is a great thought, but one that we can scarcely think. Yet it is true and real that the words I use in order to convey my thought to you actually have been formed by the mental striving of all men who have lived and worked on the earth. The instruments I use from day to day to do my work are a direct inheritance handed down from the first tool-maker. The ship on which I voyaged to these Western shores is

descended from the rude canoe which first made
the water that separates land from land to serve
as a way of communication. The mighty machinery of to-day which places all the resources of the
planet at the service of every man, is the fruit of
that inventive faculty displayed by the earliest workers of mankind.

These things come first to mind as we seek for
illustrations of the solidarity of man. But, while
they are the most obvious, they are not the strongest
or the most vivid of such illustrations. The emotions
of men are of the same kind from the beginning
until now. Pain and pleasure are sought and avoided
all through the ages, and desire and aversion are
still the motives which spur to action. No doubt
the experiences of the ages have enriched the contents of the emotions, if they have not changed
their character. Nor has the intellectual character
changed through the ages, however much the
settled data on which intellect works have been
increased. Man is one through all time, and the
connections between the successive generations are
exceedingly close. The first emotions, desires, affections of men have flowered and come to the fruit
they bear to-day, and the earliest experience of good
and evil has had in it the great ethical principles
which guide the action of the wisest and best to
this hour.

Nor do we find anything different as we question

the philosophies of the past and present. Long
ago appeared the materialist, the positivist, and the
idealist. The primitive man looked at the world
outside, and seemed to think of himself simply as
part of that world, determined by it, and made by
it. Ere reflection following on action taught him
to know himself as a source of energy, he regarded
himself, so far as he had thought at all, as a product
of the world outside. Nor is that way of thinking
dead yet. Uniformities of succession generate uniformities of thought, we are told, and the advocate
of that view spends volumes to prove that matter
makes mind, and necessities of matter may be transformed into mental necessities. To look at matter
as first and causal, and productive of mind, has been
always with men, and still is here, and the unity of
thinking is so far proven. But the idealist view did
not linger far behind. For soon the early man found
that he could do something and be something. He
knew himself as a worker, as one that had feelings,
desires, wants, and who could take steps to carry
out his wishes; thus the world became transformed
before his mind, and became a world figured in his
own likeness. So the great ideal philosophies took
their beginning, and these also appear perennially,
for they, too, have their roots deep down in the spiritual nature of man. From the beginning men have
asked the same questions, and they will continue to
ask them to the end. The answers to these ques-

tions make up the science, the ethics, the philosophy, and the theology of the world.

I deal with the questions and the answers in order to illustrate the theme I have in hand, namely, the unity of man. However great the advance that has been made, however wide our knowledge, and however great our command over the forces of nature, the advance itself is a testimony to the unity of that human nature to which it is due. Physically, morally, and intellectually man is one. We shall not find the union to be constituted, as the organism is constituted, by physical bonds. To understand the unity of man in any adequate way, we must transcend the physical and the visible, and seek the bond of union in the invisible, that is, in the intellectual, moral, and spiritual, or, to use the word which includes all these, in the rational sphere.

The demand which reason makes on reason to think humanity as a unity is confessedly great, and it is difficult to say whether we can think it so. It is difficult to think of the past generations of men in their concrete reality; it is difficult to think the people living in their concrete reality at the present hour, and it is scarcely possible to realize at all the generations yet to be. When we try to realize the past, we break it up into histories of nations, of institutions, of philosophies, of religions, and so on, and perhaps that is the best we can do. But we ought to remember that all these histories are only aspects of the great reality that has been, and has been acted in sorrow, trial, and suffering in the lives and acts of men on this round earth. At all events, this thought should make us a little more humble, a little less sure as to the conclusions we draw from our reasonings and philosophies — the unity of man is there whether we can think it or no. And in a measure we can think it, at least so far as to recognize that it is there.

We may rise to the magnitude of the thought slowly and gradually. From the family to the tribe, from the tribe to the city, from the state-city to the state, from the state to the great federal union, and from the great federal union to the federation of the world, and to the recognition of the fact that God has made of one blood all the nations of the earth. In some way we must rise to this magnitude if we are to understand the problem which we set to ourselves. It is easier to grasp the lesser unities in our thought, and to apprehend the significance of the family and so on; but our thought cannot rest until we recognize the larger unity in which these lesser unities are. Nor can we recognize fully our own significance as moral beings existing here and now, unless we see in a measure our relations to all the rational beings which have been and shall be. It is the business of reason to realize relations and to act on the recognition of them. Nor will the recognition of these invisible but real bonds which bind us to the past of humanity be without influence on our thought, character, and conduct.

I am aware that in this contention of mine I am running the risk of contradiction by many of our foremost workers in philosophy. Professor Wallace says: "The rule for man is not merely to accept the given, but to mould and fashion it for himself. In him nothing merely is; it is to be; it has taken on it a new law, the law of becoming, as the law which governs him and the things he deals with. With his emergence on the scene, the world has, as it were, got a new relative centre; all things have become, or, rather, are more and more becoming, anthropocentric." ("Natural Theology and Ethics," p. 112.) Professor James, of Harvard, to whom we all owe so much, for he has shown how philosophy may also be literature, says, in an oft-quoted passage, which also he has quoted from himself: "We have no organ or faculty to appreciate the simply given order. The real world as it is given objectively at this moment is the sum total of all its beings and events now. But can we think of such a sum? Can we realize for an instant what a cross-section of all existence at a definite point of time would be? While I talk and the flies buzz, a sea-gull catches a sea fish at the mouth of the Amazon, a tree falls in the Adirondack wilderness, a man sneezes in Germany, a horse dies in Tartary, and twins are born in France. What does that mean? Does the contemporaneity of these events with one another, and with a million others as disjointed, form a rational bond between them, and unite them into anything that means for us a world? Yet such a collateral contemporaneity, and nothing else, is the real order of the world. It is an order with which we have nothing to do but to get away from it as fast as possible. As I said, we break it; we break it into histories, and we break it into arts, and we break it into sciences; and then we begin to feel at home." ("The Will to Believe," pp. 118–9.) President Hyde quotes the passage from Professor James and adds: "The passage from Professor James shows that the world in which we live is a construction made by the mind in the interest of the heart and will: and that ·in this one great world there are subordinate worlds of history, science, and art. It shows how utterly unintelligible and uninhabitable and unendurable a real as opposed to an ideal world would be; and that practical idealism is simply a presentation of the familiar facts of everyday life in their rational relations, as elements in a logical process and parts of an organic whole." ("Practical Idealism," pp. 5–6.) Mr. Herbert Spencer has a passage in which he enumerates a number of simultaneous occurrences happening at the same moment, and his inference is that the unknowable power must be something higher than intelligence, for no intelligence could endure so heavy a strain. Thus from Hegelians, Non-Hegelians, and agnostics there is a consensus of opinion which seems to condemn my argument as it has been set forth up to this time.

I find myself in agreement with these authorities in so far as they set forth the necessity under which we lie as to the breaking up of things, and the fact that the world we live in is constituted by our own activity. We do and we must break up things; but then we do and we must unite the breakages into a unity again, and make them as like the original unity as we can. In fact, Professor James does this very thing himself in the sequel to the passage we have quoted. "We make ten thousand separate serial orders of it, and on any one of these we react as though the others did not exist. We discover among its various parts relations that were never given to sense at all (mathematical relations, tangents, squares, and roots, and logarithmic functions), and out of an infinite number of these we call certain ones essential and lawgiving, and ignore the rest. Essential these relations are, but only *for our purpose*, the other relation being just as real and present as they, and our purpose is to *conceive simply* and to *foresee*. Are not simple conception and prevision subjective ends pure and simple? They are the ends of what we call science; and the miracle of miracles —a miracle not yet exhaustively cleared up by any philosophy — is that the given order lends itself to the remodelling. It shows itself plastic to many of our scientific, to many of our æsthetic, to

many of our practical purposes and ends." (pp.
119–20.)

It is a striking paragraph, eloquently and felici-
tously expressed, and yet a great deal is implied in
it which has not found expression. The thousand
separate serial orders can be made by us, because
there is one order lying at the basis of them, as the
condition of their possibility. If some seem to respond, as we react on them, as if the others do not
exist, the response is not complete, but measured
and conditioned by the others, and we, perhaps, unconsciously, make allowance in our reaction for their
existence and their influence. Illustrations of this
have been given already, and we need not repeat
them here. I confess that it is difficult to follow
Professor James when he asks, " Are not simple
conception and prevision subjective ends pure and
simple?" What, then, becomes of the objectivity of
science, and of the fact that nature will carry out our
purpose, if we can intelligently instruct her to do so?
We at once get back the objectivity of science in the
miracle of miracles which no philosophy has yet exhaustively cleared up. The given order lends itself
to the remodelling. Yes, but that is only one-half
of the story. The remodelling would do well to lend
itself to the given order.

In truth, there seems to lie at the basis of the view
of Professor James a kind of belief that there is an
irrational, contingent, and irreducible element in the

given order. Hence the way in which he piles up the number of events which happen contemporaneously all over the world, which we cannot reduce to any order. The number might be indefinitely increased, and the impression made by them might also be multiplied. It is quite true that we have to make our selection out of the actualities of the world, if we are to understand its ongoing at all. But the talk goes on as if the world were unintelligible until we came into it. We speak as if we constitute the order of the world, and as if the rationality of the world depended on our remodelling of it. I venture humbly but emphatically to enter my dissent. The thousand serial separate orders which we make of the world are possible because the relations are there already, and, while in a sense we make them, we in a truer sense simply recognize them. How is it that our separate serial orders are always undergoing reconstruction, and our histories of science, literature, art, philosophy, need ever to be rewritten, if it were not for the necessity of bringing our serial orders into closer conformity to the given order?

Take the works of science, and let us ask ourselves what is their history? Is it not true that the greatest and most severe critic of science is just the given order? The conceptions of physics and chemistry have been recast within our own time. The old terminology has almost passed into abeyance, and the talk now is in terms of energy and evolution. The world of science presents another aspect at the end of this century from that which it ever had before. If it is the business of science to conceive simply and to foresee, then it fulfils that function more completely than before. Why? Because it tries to see the thing and its working as they are in the given order. It tries to see, as Clerk Maxwell said in his youth, the "particular go" of the thing. There is a standard and a goal for science, and that standard would seem to be the recognition and the statement of the rationality of the given order.

While this is true of the physical sciences, it is still more true of the sciences which deal with man. In those sciences, we have to deal not only with the immanent rationality of the world, which manifests itself as irreversible and irresistible order, but with the manifestations of finite intelligence which is on the way to realize itself. Histories of knowledge, ethics, philosophy, and religion deal, as one might say, with rationality in the making. The making of a finite rational being seems to be a long and costly work. Account is to be taken of the ultimate rationality of the world, and also of the tentative efforts of the finite being who has to make his own world. But we should never be able to make the worlds in which we dwell, in each of which there is a centre and circumference relative to the individual, if there were not in each of us a trust that in the larger world, which includes the separate serial worlds, there is a rationality as much greater than ours as the real world is greater than our ideal worlds.

Each of us is equal to the world which we have constructed for ourselves. Everything in that world is relative to the person who was active in the making of it. May we not suppose a rational intelligence for which the world is, and to which all the simultaneous and successive changes may be present as really as the world of our experience is to ourselves? May not the given order be the rational order after all, and our serial editions of it be simply attempts after something not yet seen by us? At all events the statement that the real is the rational is a proposition for which a good deal may be said.

So we come back to our proposition that we must strive to rise to the thought of the wider and wider unities that meet us as we read the unfolding history of the world. We must try to think things together, and not merely in the separate serials presented to us for our easier reading. We must try to think things together, for they are together. Our serials may be useful and profitable reading, if we remember that they must be bound together and read together if we are to reach the goal. Even then they must be read only as approximations to the great reality. The great order of the world has made room for the order which a rational being constructs for himself within it; it would be strange if the rational being were to conclude that there was no reason in the world until he put it there. The response which the world makes to our intelligent efforts, the plasticity of the world under our remodelling hand, looks as if provision were made in the nature of things for the advent of such a being as man. At all events, it is true that a rational being has found a place in the system of things, and has room and freedom to work there.

The race of rational beings has lived and worked here for a long time, and has left traces of themselves and their work. They have transformed the place in which they have lived, have made for themselves a home in it. The fruits of the earth have been modified to meet their wants, the plants have taken on new forms to gratify their taste and to feed and clothe them, the winds of heaven serve their pleasure, fire has become their servant, and the lightnings carry their messages. Cities have risen at their command, and, while they have subdued the earth to their purpose, they have themselves grown from more to more. They have worked on the same lines from the first to the last, only with an intelligence that has grown with the demand made on it. They have left the record of their hopes, fears, beliefs, aims, and purposes, and have enabled us to see how they looked on the heavens above, and the earth beneath; what they thought of the past, the present, and the future. We know how they regarded the great mystery of existence, and we can read their growing apprehension of the greatness of the world in which they lived. Is it any wonder that we are constrained to think of them as a unity?

Here, too, may come forth considerations similar to those which Professor James set forth in another connection. We may be told that we have no organ to grasp so large a unity. If we cannot grasp the contemporaneity, how shall we grasp the contemporaneity and the succession, too? And yet it must somehow be grasped, for we all recognize it as a fact. If we begin with any unity in which we may imagine ourselves to be placed, we shall find ourselves pushed in thought on and on till we are face to face with the whole race as they have existed in space and in time. Our thought refuses to be shut up in compartments. Begin where we stand with any individual now present, and from him we shall be thrust forth to the thought of this great city, and of all the complex relations which make up the history and the present constitution of this city. From the city we shall be driven in thought to the state, and to the great nation of which it forms an integral part. Then our thought will find no resting place until we think of the relations of this state to the other states of the world. You cannot write a history of the United States without a glance at the

countries on the other side from which your fore-
fathers came; you cannot explain your ethics, philosophy, religion, without regard to the rock whence
you are hewn, and the ancestral traits you carried
with you to your home here. No doubt you have
also made your own contribution to the thought
and life of men — a contribution which grows larger
every day.

The matter in hand is that you cannot begin
anywhere without assuming in your thought the
whole history of mankind. And you cannot continue thinking to any purpose without the postulate
of the larger unity of the human race which underlies all your thinking. It may not have come
clearly before your consciousness, but as soon as it
is pointed out, we all recognize that it has been
the tacit assumption of all of us. So I am not to
be debarred from the use of this unity of man by
any difficulty which may be brought against my
power adequately to conceive it. Difficulties as
great, and, in the opinion of some, as insuperable,
can be brought against the conception of any unity
whatsoever. You have only to read "Appearance
and Reality," by Mr. F. H. Bradley, to find as fine
an assortment of difficulties as can be found in
any place in the world. The difficulties are perplexing enough, whether you speak of time, or space,
or self, or of anything else which you think as
one. In this related world you can never take a

thing out of its relations, for, as soon as you bring in the relations, it may be shown that you have broken up the unity. It may be shown that you have no right to speak of the weight of any particular body, for when you do, you are simply speaking of a relation which this particular thing has to all the things which make up the universe. In fact, difficulties arise when we speak of any unity in which differences occur, and which is made up of differences. There is no greater inherent difficulty in thinking of a unity made up of many differences, than there is in thinking of a unity made up of a few.

It is quite true that thought cannot rest until it reaches a final unity in which all existence finds its place, which will, also, give to every difference a place and a function in the unity of all. Thought ever tends that way, and many have been the attempts made to find a unity of that kind. We are not yet ready for the consideration of these. We are familiarizing ourselves with the wider and wider unities which have met our view as we followed the history of the world set forth to us by science. We have come in man to a new kind of unity, which in many ways has transcended those we met before. Not merely an organic unity, nor a mechanical unity held together by pressure, but a unity of independent, self-guided, rational beings, held together by an inward motive, and bound by bonds which are moral and spiritual. Constituted for each individual by descent, tradition, upbringing, education, family, and social intercourse, it has to be constituted anew by him of his own choice and rational desire. Into that union the individual has to bring himself with all that has been given him, and all that he has made himself to be; and he has to find himself, as he can find himself only, in the society. It is open to him to refuse to enter into the unity of humanity on the terms which alone can make the union beneficial to the society and to himself. He may in a short-sighted and irrational way refuse the wider outlook, disregard the limitations and restraints, which the good of the whole has laid on the individual; he may look at all things from an individual standpoint; he may use the means provided by the labour of the generations for what he thinks his own benefit, and the strength, skill, and power he owes to society may be turned against it: these considerations only show how difficult it is to constitute a rational unity out of individuals who are only partially rational, and have not become rational enough to know wherein their highest interests lie.

At this point emerge other considerations on which we have not touched as yet. We have to consider the beliefs of humanity from a point of view which throws into relief another aspect of man. If the ideal of humanity is higher than we have yet seen, if we have to look at man as continuing in existence beyond this world of time, if we are to regard the members of the human race as living at this hour, somewhere, after they have passed from this life, clearly our conception of the unity of humanity receives a breadth unspeakably great. If we continue to live on, and if the other life is in connection with the present life, then the relation of the individual to the unity of humanity assumes a new form, and the bonds of union become still more spiritual than before. We feel at once that we are members of a larger whole, and the responsibility to the whole assumes a graver aspect. Whatever we do here has an eternal aspect. We are ourselves transformed under the grander, deeper light, and our feelings, desires, aims, thoughts, have a deeper meaning, for we recognize that we are not the children of time.

It may be asked whether at this stage we have not passed beyond rational grounds, and have brought to light hopes or fears which reason cannot verify. It has been contended that reason has to do only with the present world and the present life, and to go beyond these is to bring in what passes the bounds of verification. Precisely as it has been contended that reason has only to do with the interests of the individual, so it has been contended that it has to do only with the present life. Both these propositions have been advocated by Mr. Kidd in his work on "Social Evolution," and it seems right to look at his argument. Meanwhile, let us observe that even if we limit our view to the present life, and to the disclosures of history, it is clear that the bonds between the individual and society are of the most real and practical kind. We can discover these bonds, can discern these conditions; indeed, they have been discovered and set forth, so that he who runs may read. The relations are as real as those set forth in physics, and the sanctions for social conduct are as real and as conspicuous as those which dictate a regard to the welfare of the individual. But it may be well to hear what Mr. Kidd has to say on the subject, and to discuss the matter with him at some length.

VI

IS A RATIONAL RELIGION POSSIBLE? MR. BENJAMIN KIDD AND MR. ARTHUR BALFOUR

IT may be well to begin with a quotation from the work of Mr. Benjamin Kidd on " Social Evolution." That book has had a great vogue with us, and it seems also to have attracted attention on this side of the Atlantic. Its recognition of the part which religion has in social evolution, its insistence on the altruistic character of social morality, and the courageous maintenance of the proposition that the hope of humanity lay in the development of religious feeling and of the conduct that springs therefrom, won the approval of all who felt the need of religious sanctions for the guidance of their own lives. They were so much entranced with the clear and emphatic insistence of the necessity of religion for man, that they forgot to ask whether a religion was possible on the terms and within the limits prescribed by Mr. Kidd. As I read the book and watched the reception given to it, I came to the conclusion that the Aufklärung was not yet dead. Here was a book with all the notes of

the Aufklärung, with the tendency of the Aufklärung
to shut up nature and human nature into compartments, and to introduce discord and anarchy into
the separate compartments, that placed religion and
morality out of rational relation with one another,
and pitted religion against rationality so far as to say
that a rational religion is impossible ; and yet the book
was praised beyond measure, and edition after edition
was rapidly sold.

I was reminded of Henry Thomas Buckle and
his " History of Civilization."   The two men and the
two books were not unlike each other.   They dealt
largely with the same problem and they used the
same method.   It is true that the principle of progress to which the advance of civilization is due is
not the same, but in both the principle is one-sided,
and in both it proceeds on the assumption of a radical
contradiction in human nature.   The principle of
progress is with Mr. Buckle intellectual; with Mr.
Kidd it is extra-rational.   With Mr. Buckle religion,
at least in its historical manifestations, is superstitious, irrational, and a hindrance to progress; with
Mr. Kidd it is also extra-rational, irrational, but a
help, indeed the only help to progress.   Cultivate
the intelligence, enlighten the mind, spread the light
of knowledge everywhere, and the millennium is
sure to come, so spoke the earlier prophet, as he pero-
rated with such eloquence as he could command on
the advance of the species, and contrasted the past

with the present. The prophet of the present tells
a different story. Enlightenment is not increasing,
and it would not be good for the human race if it did
increase. The human mind has not grown throughout the ages, for was not a Greek as intelligent as we
are? There is no rational sanction for progress, for
the secret of progress lies in the unintelligible and
the irrational. Let us struggle to overcome our own
reason, and let us subordinate it to the irrational, so
shall we hasten the wheels of progress and advance
civilization.

Thus we have in both writers the essential principle of the Aufklärung, — the splitting up of man into
unrelated factors, the rupture of the unity of intelligence, the assumption that essential and related
parts of human nature are in entire antagonism to
one another; and the consequence follows that they
must brand that part they do not use, and cast it out
as an intruder, and a disturber of the peace and progress of humanity. It is quite an accident that Mr.
Buckle regards religion as the intruder, and Mr.
Kidd looks on reason, in his sense of the word, as the
enemy; for the positions might be reversed and the
same result would follow. I for one protest against
the breaking up of the mind into separate faculties
that in the phraseology of some seem to act inde-
pendently of one another, and against that assumption that the manifold of sense has to wait till it is
gathered up into the unity of apperception; and I

protest, also, against the introduction into philosophy of phraseology which will prevent me from seeing that feeling, thinking, acting, is done by the whole being, and is not a series of unrelated processes conducted by abstractions.

Let us, however, hear Mr. Kidd. " This orderly and beautiful world which we see around us is now, and always has been, the scene of incessant rivalry between all the forms of life inhabiting it — rivalry, too, not chiefly conducted between different species, but between members of the same species. The plants in the green-sward beneath our feet are engaged in silent rivalry with each other, a rivalry which if allowed to proceed without outside interference would know no pause until the weaker were exterminated. Every plant, organ, or quality of these plants which calls forth admiration for its beauty or perfection has its place and meaning in this struggle, and has been acquired to ensure success therein. The trees of the forest which clothe and beautify the landscape are in a state of nature engaged in the same rivalry with each other. Left to themselves they fight out, as unmistakable records have shown, a stubborn struggle extending over centuries in which at last only those forms most suitable to the conditions of the locality retain their places. But so far we view the rivalry under simple conditions; it is amongst the forms of animal life as we begin to watch the gradual progress upwards to higher types that it becomes many sided and complex.

It is at this point that we encounter a feature of the struggle which recent developments of biological science tend to bring into ever increasing prominence. The first necessity for every successful form engaged in this struggle is the capacity for reproduction beyond the limits which the conditions of life for the time being comfortably provide for. The capacity for multiplying in this way is at first one of the principal resources in the development upwards, and in the lower forms of life it is still almost the sole equipment. But as progress begins to be made, a deeper cause, the almost illimitable significance of which science is beginning to appreciate, requires that all the successful forms must multiply beyond the limits of comfortable existence.

Recent biological researches, and more particularly the investigations and conclusions of Professor Weismann, have tended to greatly develop Darwin's original hypothesis as to the conditions under which progress has been made in the various forms of life. It is now coming to be recognized as a necessarily inherent part of the doctrine of evolution that, if the continual selection which is always going on amongst the higher forms of life were to be suspended, these forms would not only possess no tendency to make progress; they must actually go backwards. *That is to say, if all the individuals of every generation in any species were allowed to equally propagate their kind, the average of each generation would con-*

tinually tend to fall below the average of the genera-tion which preceded it, and a process of slow but steady degeneration would ensue." ("Social Evolution," pp. 38–9.)

We have quoted at length, as the quotation sets forth one of the main elements of Mr. Kidd's argument. At the outset we notice the stress he lays on struggle. Rivalry everywhere, cell against cell, part against part, organism against organism, species against species, and genus against genus. It is set forth in the most extreme and one-sided way, with utter blindness to the other side of the story. There is no word of that which made the so-called struggle possible, and no thought of the fact that every species is serviceable to every other. Nor is there any mention that the plant life must precede animal life, in order to lift matter to that chemical level at which it may become the vehicle of animal life. Nor is there any regard to the fact that the various species of animals depend on one another to a degree which passes calculation. The soil on which corn is grown has been worked over and over again, until it has attained that condition which makes it fit for the growing of corn. In truth, Mr. Kidd, following his masters, has isolated one set of phenomena, fixed his thought on it exclusively, until he has quite forgotten that, if there be a struggle, it is a struggle within one system.

Nor has he observed that the higher the organism

the less the fertility. On this Mr. Spencer has written much that is to the purpose, and has gone far to prove that there is a law of fertility. But then Mr. Spencer, though a thorough-going evolutionist, is, unlike Mr. Kidd, a disbeliever in the adequacy of natural selection. Mr. Kidd says grandly, "Amongst the higher forms it is an inevitable law not only that competition and selection must always accompany progress, but that they must prevail amongst every form of life which is not actually retrograding. Every successful form must, of necessity, multiply beyond the limits which the average conditions of life comfortably provide for. Other things being equal, indeed, the wider the limits of selection the keener the rivalry, and the more rigid the selection the greater will be the progress." (p. 41.) It is so easy to make general statements, and to speak of inevitable laws, and yet the greater part of Mr. Kidd's book is taken up with a proof that the success of humanity as a social system is due to the fact that men have somehow disregarded the stern competition and rivalry which he speaks of with so strong an emphasis. No wonder that he regards such conduct as irrational. But of this more in the sequel.

We note further the adherence of Mr. Kidd to the opinion of Weismann. In his usual fashion he speaks of Weismann's view, as if it had been accepted by those who know. He might have told us which of

Weismann's views he holds by, for Weismann has set forth at least half a dozen different ones. But take the one Mr. Kidd has chosen, and on which he dilates at some length. It is scarcely possible to follow the reasoning of Weismann and the elaboration of that reasoning by Mr. Kidd. They make the strange supposition of the cessation of natural selection. In one breath they tell us that this is the law of life and progress, and then calmly speak of its cessation, and seek to trace out its consequences. It seems to me that I could make the supposition of the cessation of gravitation, and on that supposition trace out a good many consequences of an inconvenient kind. Really they must make their choice. Natural selection is universal or it is not. It seems to me that it is universal in the sense that there must be a correspondence between the organism and its environment. The fittest must survive whatever the fittest may be. The survival tests the fitness. To speak from the standpoint of evolution of "a process of slow but steady degeneration" is to go beyond the mark, and to bring in a standard not derived from evolution.

The stress and strain of rivalry and competition may work for progress, or may work for degradation. Change the environment of this place a few degrees, and lower it on the average until it became what it is in the Arctic regions, and the fittest would survive, but it would be a different kind of fitness. What we may call a degraded form would inevitably

be the outcome of such a state of matters. It is
noticeable that Mr. Kidd makes another assumption
which he has not attempted to justify. He simply
asserts it as indubitable. Assuming for the sake of
examining his proposition on its merits, that the cessation of natural selection is possible, why does he
assume that the result would be degeneration? Underlying the assumption is the thought, never expressed, but always understood, that variation would
cease, or that the organism would vary only in one
direction. How does this assumption agree with the
hypothesis of indefinite variation? This is one of the
points which have emerged in the controversy between Weismann and Spencer, on which Spencer
lays great stress, and to which Weismann has given
no satisfactory answer. If, as Mr. Kidd says, "the
higher forms of life would tend to sink back again by
a degenerative process through those stages of development by which they reached their present position,"
this could only be characterized from the standpoint of
evolution as a case of the survival of the fittest. In
truth, one gets a little tired of this kind of argument,
and one wishes for a little consistency of thought and
of adherence to one point of view for a time. Mr.
Kidd cannot eat his cake and have it. If he is to use
the language and to unfold the arguments of evolution, he has no right to speak of degeneration, for
that is to bring in another measure than that used by
evolution. He can only speak of the survival of the

fittest, and whatever survives is the fittest.　Thus his talk about progress is swept away, as being beyond the sphere to which judgment is limited by the premises.

Greater wonders meet us as we follow on in the perusal of Mr. Kidd's book.　He brings the laws of biology to the interpretation of human life; he makes no discrimination between the more involved life to which he comes and the less involved life he has previously studied, and we rather expect that he will soon get into difficulties.　Even in the lower life he has refused to look at anything save rivalry, competition, and the struggle for existence.　He has refused to look at the tenderness and devotion of a mother to her little ones, and there are such among animals.　He has not noticed union and subordination to their leader of a herd of grass-eaters, nor how they work together for their common advantage. These herds set sentinels to watch while others feed; they obey the signal of their leaders.　If there are struggle and suffering, there are among animals love, gentleness, care for their young, and the germs of many virtues which in flower and fruit are the glory of humanity.　These have been omitted from Mr. Kidd's picture.

Biology has to be widened and narrowed when we come to look at the being who has become rational.　In a sense, our author recognizes a difference between rational and irrational beings.　He carries with him, however, the idea that "no form can make any advance, or even retain its place without deterioration, except by carrying on the species to a greater extent from individuals above the average than from those below it," and makes the problem presented to the rational being to be, what shall his behaviour be under the onerous conditions of his existence. It is only fair to let him state his case: "Here at last was a creature who could reason about these things and who, when his conduct is observed, it may be noticed, actually does reason about them in this way. He is subject to the same natural conditions of existence as all the forms of life that have come before him; he reproduces his kind as they do; he lives and dies subject to the same physiological laws. To him, as to the others, the inexorable conditions of life render progress impossible in any other way than by carrying on his kind from successful variations to the exclusion of others; by being therefore subject to selection; by consequently reproducing in numbers beyond those which the conditions of life for the time being comfortably allow for; and by living a life of constant rivalry and competition with his fellows with all the attendant results of stress and suffering to some, and failure to reach the full possibilities of life to large numbers. Nay, more, it is evident that his progress has become subject to these conditions in a more stringent and onerous form than has ever before prevailed in the world. For as he can reach his highest development only in society, the forces which are concerned in working out his evolution no longer operate upon him primarily as an individual, but as a member of society. His interests as an individual have, in fact, become further subordinated to those of a social organism, with interests immensely wider and a life indefinitely longer than his own. How is the possession of reason ever to be rendered compatible with the will to submit to conditions of existence so onerous, requiring the effective and continual subordination of the individual's welfare to the progress of a development in which he can have no personal interest whatever." (pp. 68–9.)

This is his statement of the problem, and we shall look at it as stated, or we may take it as set forth by himself in all the dignity of italics. "*The interests of the social organism and those of the individuals comprising it at any particular time are actually antagonistic; they can never be reconciled; they are inherently and essentially irreconcilable.*" So we get the matter at last with all the breadth and absoluteness characteristic of the Aufklärung. The social organism becomes an abstraction on the one side, and the individuals comprising it become abstractions on the other, and the whole contents of both for the time are just this opposition which has also been abstracted from all else. Apparently the author has forgotten that if the individuals comprising the social organism disappear, the organism disappears also, and with the disappearance of the organism goes all that gave the individual his significance. It might just as reasonably be said that "the interest of the social organism and those of the individuals comprising it at any particular time can never be separated, they can never be antagonistic, they are inherently and essentially inseparable." As an axiom, ours is as good as his, and it has the advantage of being more consistent with the facts.

Without the social organism the individual could not be, and certainly could not be what he is. Take him as he stands in New York to-day, and let the stress of competition be as great as you please, see how you have equipped the individual for his work. At his command you have placed the gift of common speech which unites him with his fellows, and places at his service the immense tradition of the experience of men in all ages and climes. You have trained and educated him in your schools, and have placed at his service the trained intelligence of men and women who can help him in the task of unfolding his powers, and of enabling him to know the world in which he lives, and of making it realize his purposes. You place at his command the resources of all that the industry of former times has accumulated, all that the inventive power of all time has discovered, and as he grows up he has at his breakfast table the news of the world. It is really not necessary to multiply instances of the service which the social organism has done in the making of the individual.

He is trained and fitted for his work by the social organism, and not merely intellectually; he has had his affections drawn forth, his social qualities developed in daily intercourse with his fellows, and his moral and religious nature has been strengthened by his place in, and by the part he has taken in, the moral and religious institutions in which he has been brought up. So far intellectually, morally, and religiously he has had the opportunity of making himself, in interaction with his fellows in the social organism. It is not too much to say that to-day in your country and in ours, the resources of civilization place at the command of our workingmen opportunities which kings could not command a thousand years ago. But, says Mr. Kidd, the social organism lays on the individuals comprising it onerous burdens for which there is no rational sanction. Yes, onerous burdens are laid on every man. It is the law of life that man must be a worker, and only in work can he realize himself. But that law does not lead us to the partial conclusion of Mr. Kidd.

A rational sanction! what does Mr. Kidd mean by the phrase and what does he mean by the word "reason"? It is one of the puzzles of his book. We are surprised as we find that the only function ascribed by him to reason, is that it is a power which enables the individual to look after his own interest. It enabled him to overcome his competitors in the struggle for existence, and the possessor of reason subdued the irrational animals. It enabled him to discover that the onerous conditions of existence still continued as they were before his advent. Still reason did not throw these off, for it was circumvented by another set of instincts — shall we call them so? — which serve the social organism, and help man to subordinate his own reason. So in this artificial way Mr. Kidd tries to repair the rupture which he himself had made. Reason with him simply means reasoning, the power of breaking up, analyzing, of seeing separate particulars, and of dwelling on these exclusively. It can discover the onerous obligations of existence laid on the individual, and can see that these are irreconcilable with those of the social organism. He protests that "the terms 'reason' and 'rational' are here, as everywhere throughout this book, used in their ordinary or natural sense, and not in that transcendent sense in which metaphysicians toward the end of the last century set the fashion of using them." (p. 73.)

Suppose we use the word in his sense, we have still to contend that he has unduly limited the scope of reason. For reason is able to recognize, not only the fact that it is under onerous obligations, as regards the work the individual has to do; it is, also, able to recognize all the conditions under which men exist on the earth, and to shape its course accordingly. It can recognize that the individual is no mere individual, and that when he endeavours to separate his own interests from those of the social organism, he is acting irrationally. To limit reason as Mr. Kidd has done, is to set down a limit that does not exist, save in his own imagination. For man is set here under a number of conditions, in a certain number of relations, and he has to know, as far as he can, these conditions and relations. Through these he has to realize himself, live his life, and do his work. It is the business of reason to ascertain all these conditions and relations, and not merely some of them. The relations that bind him to society are real and rational relations, and the observance of them are for the interest of the individual. So on his own ground we say again to Mr. Kidd that to regard the interests of the society and the individual as irreconcilable is an irrational proceeding.

In truth, according to Mr. Kidd, we are in a world that is fundamentally and utterly irrational. There is no rational sanction for the conditions of existence necessarily existing, there is no possibility of a rational religion, and the universe is one in which irrational procedure seems to be the rule. Yet science has gone to work on the supposition that the world was intelligible, and found that it was so. And men have lived and acted on the assumption that things have a law, and a meaning, if they could find that law and meaning, and they thought they had found both in some measure; but here comes Mr. Kidd with the discovery that in the highest of all the phenomena in the world the conditions of existence have no rational sanction. It is very wonderful, and it has been discovered by the reason of Mr. Kidd. It must have been a sad thing to find out that reason is without kith or kin in this wide universe, and that this solitary endowment is unable to bring the conditions of existence into harmony with itself, or itself with them. At this stage it might have occurred to Mr. Kidd to retrace his steps, and to try to find out whether this contrariety in the very centre of life did exist. He might have asked whether his abstraction of the individual from the social organism had not been carried to an extreme.

It is easy to make abstractions, easy to split up the individual into faculties, and to place one mode of the action of a being into irreconcilable contradiction with another, if we lose sight of the unity which really conditions all the actions of every creature. But on the whole we may say that that mode of procedure has been overdone. We may say, also, that it has been overdone in the more recent study of the relations of the individual and society. It does not work to sink the individual in the social organism, or to do the reverse. The individual can only realize himself in the organism, and the organism suffers when the individual is kept from realizing his ideal. Reason has a higher work than that assigned to it by Mr. Kidd. It has to seek to know all the relations in which rational beings stand to one another in the social organism; the relations also in which they all stand to the world beneath them, and to what is above them all, and to define the rational constitution of the world in view of all these relations as a rational system, at least as a system that can be thought. For any individual to look merely at himself, at his work, at the conditions under which he does his work, to disregard all other interests save those which seem to belong to the individual for the moment, is possible for an individual, but only if he disregards the wider unity which alone can render his life and work fruitful. To speak of reason as if it meant an instrument only for the advantage of the individual, or as if it could not discern any other or wider bond, is to degrade the name and to do violence to the ordinary use of language. Reason is eminently social, and can make use of society for its own growth and further realization. Instead of limiting reason to the function to which it is reduced by Mr. Kidd, it would be more consonant to fact to widen its use and to make it coterminous with all the activity of a rational being.　Looking at the rational being, we see the coming of the time when all the feelings, emotions, desires, all the knowledge, and all the voluntary activity of the rational being will be suffused with reason, and all will move in harmony with the ideal set forth by reason as the goal to be reached by each and all.

As Mr. Kidd has unduly limited the use of reason, and made it only an instrument for the benefit of the individual, so he has also unduly narrowed the sphere of religion.　He has recognized in a very vivid way the influence of religion in the progress of man, and he has set it forth in such a way as to call attention to it, when it was rather neglected by writers on evolution.　It was looked at as altogether superstitious, as injurious, and as a hindrance to the progress of civilization.　But Mr. Kidd is emphatic in his statement of its power and its worth as the instrument of social progress.　But he seems to us to leave out of the conception many elements which are necessary to the very idea of a religion.　Here is his definition : *A religion is a form of belief, providing an ultra-rational sanction for that large class of conduct in the individual where his interests and the interests of the social organism are antagonistic, and by which the former are rendered subordinate to the latter in the general interests of the evolution which the race is undergoing.* (p. 112.)

This is a description of religion simply by one of

its effects.   It tells us nothing of religion as a belief in a power higher than ourselves on whom we feel our dependence, nothing of the necessity for fellowship with that power, nothing of what seems to disturb that fellowship, and of how it is to be restored, nor does it say anything of the commandments of the power. Every religion that has appeared among men has had its beliefs, its commands, and its consolations. These, however, do not appear in the definition of Mr. Kidd. His definition seems to have been prescribed by the necessities of his system.   He had found that there was no rational sanction for progress, he must therefore provide an irrational sanction, for the existence of progress is a fact.   Religion is the instrument by which the blank is supplied.   Our contention is that religion could not accomplish the task he assigns to it, if it did not accomplish a great deal more.   It has the power he assigns to it, it does give us an ideal of unselfish living and working, but it does not limit itself to that.

Indeed, the first work of an adequate religion is to restore the synthesis which Mr. Kidd has arbitrarily ruptured and cannot get together again.   One of its chief ethical commands is, " Love thy neighbour as thyself."   That is to say, that for religion the self-regarding virtues are not unimportant.   It is as much interested in those things that make for the true interests of the self, as it is in those that make for the interests of the social organism.   It does not subordinate individuals to the race, and it does not hesitate to say, "What shall it profit a man though he should gain the whole world and lose his own soul?" The highest form of religion known to man is distinctive in this respect, and is clearly distinguished from other religions in the stress it lays on the value and the worth of the individual, on the necessity of developing the individual to the height of the ideal which he only can realize, and on that distinct peculiarity which makes every person almost a type by himself. Religion is the greatest power in the universe for the making of the individual, for the insistence on every help which can tend to develop the distinctive personality of each; in fact, there is no power known to man that works so much to develop the personality of the individual as religion. This fact is altogether lost sight of by Mr. Kidd.

Religion does not work by setting the interests of the individual against those of the race. Ye are members one of another. In fact, religion was first in the field, before science, before philosophy came to being; and it had made in its own way that synthesis which science and philosophy have not yet made, after ages of toil. Somehow it grasped the whole in its wholeness, raised men up beyond the limited and the imperfect, outran its own powers of thinking, and gave to man such a sense of his own worth, and of the worth of others, as even in the imperfect forms, it had long ago, made man somewhat of an ideal being.

Religion has no such limited function as that prescribed to it by Mr. Kidd.   It is not an instrument in
the general interests of the evolution which the race
is undergoing.   It is something greater than that.   It
is in the interest of the individual quite as much.

In a page, previous to his treatment of religion, Mr.
Kidd, in a simple and artless manner, says, " We are
speaking, it must be remembered, of a rational sanction, and reason has, in an examination of this kind,
nothing to do with any existence but the present,
which it insists it is our duty to ourselves to make the
most of." (pp. 72–3.) We need not be surprised that
he says later, " No form of belief is capable of functioning as a religion in the evolution of society which
does not provide an ultra-rational sanction for social
conduct in the individual.   In other words, a rational
religion is a scientific impossibility, representing from
the nature of the case an inherent contradiction of
terms."   (pp. 109–110.)   It seems a very sad result
for the rational being.   He seems shut up to the dilemma, either to lose his rationality or to cease to be
religious.   If he follows our author, he must choose
the horn of the dilemma on which he is to be impaled.
He was wont to think that a belief in God and immortality was a belief which was justifiable on rational
grounds.   May we humbly ask why a form of belief
which provides a rational sanction for social conduct in
the individual may not be capable of functioning as a
religion in the evolution of society?   I express my own

conviction that if Mr. Kidd is right in calling "a rational religion a scientific impossibility," we shall soon see an end of religion altogether. For it is a necessity of the rational being to bring his beliefs into some kind of order, and to justify them to himself; and if you shut him out from that hope, you will drive him to despair.

After reading passages like these, — and they abound in the pages of Mr. Kidd's book, — we might expect something like a demonstration of the fundamental irrationality of religion. A statement, at least, of its opposition to the interests of the individual might be expected. As we read, we find that, whatever religion may be in itself, and whatever be the nature of its sanction, its results are intelligible, and can be stated with precision. At first we start, led by Mr. Kidd, with the notion that religion is a method of subordinating the individual and his interests to the interests of the social organism. We read on and we find that the scene is changed, and another attitude presents itself. The social organism is in the service of the individual. The social organism somehow labours not in its own interest; it works in order that all the people may be brought into the rivalry of life on equal conditions. If this be so, then all we need to do is to make this plain to the intelligence of man, the individual; and we shall immediately have a rational sanction for progress, and religion may also be regarded as rational. Lest we should be thought guilty of unfairness to Mr. Kidd, we quote the following: " Now the prevailing impression concerning this process of evolution is that it has been the product of an intellectual movement, and that it has been the ever increasing intelligence and enlightenment of the people, which has constituted the principal propelling force. It would appear, however, that we must reject this view. From the nature of the case, as we shall see more clearly later on, the intellect could not have supplied any force sufficiently powerful to have enabled the people to have successfully assailed the almost impregnable position of the power-holding classes. So enormous has been the resistance to be overcome, and so complete has been the failure of the people in similar circumstances outside our civilization, that we must look elsewhere for the cause which has produced the transformation. The motive force we must apparently find in the immense fund of altruistic feeling with which our Western societies have become equipped ; this being, with the extraordinarily effective sanctions behind it, the characteristic and determinative product of the religious system upon which our civilization is founded. *It is the influence of this fund of altruism in our civilization that has undermined the position of the power-holding classes.* It is the resulting deepening and softening of character amongst us which alone has made possible that developmental movement whereby all the people are being slowly brought into the rivalry of life on equal conditions." (p. 177.)

Surely when the average man sees that people are brought into the rivalry of life on equal conditions, and that by the effort of the social organism, he will cease to believe that there are no rational sanctions for progress, and will cease to think, if he ever did think, that his interests and the interests of the social organism are irreconcilable. It is a curious result that even Mr. Kidd should show how interests, said by him to be irreconcilable, work together for mutual advantage. We notice, in passing, a curious instance of Mr. Kidd's way of taking aspects for realities, and of making abstractions do the work which abstract notions can never do. Note how he speaks: "The intellect could not have supplied any force sufficiently powerful," and so on. An abstract intellect could not supply any force to anything, but neither could abstract feeling do it. No great movement, and no movement however insignificant, could be motived apart from the intellect, feeling, or the conations of men. To speak of a fund of altruistic feeling, as if it stood by itself, and flowed on without touching the intelligence and the will, is, with all respect, to speak psychological nonsense. But this is Mr. Kidd's way. While we are grateful to him for the service he has done in the emphasis he has laid on the power of religion in evolution, we accept that result with the qualification that religion is a reasonable service.

It may be useful here to make a few remarks on

Mr. Arthur Balfour's book — "The Foundations of Belief," as it is largely on the same lines as the book of Mr. Kidd. They agree in using the word "reason" in the same sense as simply reasoning, and they similarly lay stress on the irrational character of human beliefs. Mr. Balfour professes to deal with the foundations of belief. He seeks to ascertain the causes and the genesis of belief. For this end he dwells on the impressions made on us, on effects wrought on us, on beliefs effected in us by causes which are non-rational in themselves, and he has many wise things in his book in this connection. After the questions of the origin and growth of our beliefs have been discussed a more important question emerges, What are our beliefs worth and are they valid? and this is scarcely discussed by Mr. Balfour. Mr. Balfour approaches the question under the influence of the traditional philosophy, and has not, even though he has recognized that there is a difference between the existence of a belief and its validity, dealt with the necessity of a criterion of belief. He has shown us no way of discriminating between beliefs which are valid, trustworthy, related to reality, and those which are baseless, irrational, and degrading. As far as psychology is concerned one belief is as good as another; when its nature, its genesis, are ascertained, the work of psychology is done. English psychology always maintained the validity of the original element of mind, or the original beliefs, as Stuart Mill called them. To find what these were, it was customary to refer to that baby which has appeared so frequently in treatises of English psychology, it is fashionable now to refer to the primitive man. It has been an irrelevant procedure from first to last, for if the genesis of every belief could be traced so that we could refer every one to its adequate cause, we should still have no criterion to distinguish between beliefs as true or false. The truth or falsehood of a belief is not to be determined by a consideration of its origin, but by an examination of its contents, and the grounds offered for its acceptance. From a rational point of view a belief must be self-evident, or it must be proven, or at least its truth must appear probable. Either in itself or in its relation to other beliefs, a belief must have reasons which warrant its acceptance.

One objection to be taken to Mr. Balfour's argument is that he speaks of our beliefs as if they were mere effects wrought in us by non-rational causes. The assumption of the passivity of the mind is carried through consistently. He never looks at the possibility of the mind having a say in the matter. Our beliefs are wrought in us we know not how, and no account is taken of the nature and activity of the mind. No mental experience is a mere effect, the stimulus is reacted against in a way characteristic not of the stimulus but of the mind. But this is now so commonplace that it need not be dwelt on.

Nor does it seem necessary to speak of the contention that our beliefs are due to non-rational causes. For be the character of the causes what it may, the beliefs are beliefs of a being who is, at least, implicitly rational, and every experience of his is implicitly rational. On this I do not dwell.

Only one thing in "The Foundations of Belief" do I refer to, and I refer to it because it, also, was a favourite antithesis of the Aufklärung. "Authority and Reason" is the title of the chapter and of the antithesis in Mr. Balfour's book. "The source of error which has next to be noted presents points of much greater interest. Though it be true, as I am contending, that the importance of reason among the causes which produce and maintain the beliefs, customs, and ideals which form the groundwork of life has been much exaggerated, there can yet be no doubt that reason is, or appears to be, the cause over which we have the most direct control, or rather the one which we most readily identify with our own free and personal action. We are acted on by authority. It moulds our ways of thought in spite of ourselves, and usually unknown to ourselves. But when we reason, we are the authors of the effect produced. We have ourselves set the machine in motion. For its proper working we are ourselves immediately responsible; so that it is both natural and desirable that we should concentrate our attention on this particular class of causes, even though we should thus be led unduly to magnify their importance in the general scheme of things." ("The Foundations of Belief," p. 203.)

This is part of the general contrast between authority and reason drawn by Mr. Balfour, in which the opposition between the two is exaggerated, and their relations to one another obscured. One statement is worthy of notice. It is this, "When we reason, we are the authors of the effect produced." We are no more the authors of the effects produced by reasoning than we are the authors of our experience generally, or rather we are just as much the authors of the one as of the other. Our experience is in one sense given, in another it is constructed by our own activity. So when we reason, we construct our argument, arrange the steps of it, and seek to set forth the truth of the matter in hand; but we are not the authors of the premises or the conclusion, if these are to have an objective reference. The worth of the argument must be determined by some objective standard. In all its experiences the mind is as active as it is in reasoning. What we lay stress on is the opposition which our author supposes to exist between authority and reason. We insist on it because it is an illustration of the prevalence of that mischievous habit of the Aufklärung, which we saw prevailing so greatly in the reasoning of Mr. Kidd. Here is the same thing in Mr. Balfour, and we may find it elsewhere. "When we turn, however, from

the conscious work of Reason to that which is unconsciously performed for us by Authority, a very
different spectacle arrests our attention. The effects
of the first, prominent as they are through the dignity
of their origin, are trifling compared with the all-per-
vading influences which flow from the second. At
every moment of our lives, as individuals, as members
of a family, of a party, of a nation, of a Church, of
a universal brotherhood, the silent, continuous, un-
noticed influence of Authority moulds our feelings,
our aspirations, and, what we are more immediately
concerned with, our beliefs. It is from Authority that
Reason itself draws its most important premises."
(pp. 227–28.) The last sentence may be turned
round, and it would thus lose none of its impressiveness or its truth. It is from reason that authority
draws its most important premises. For all the institutions to which reference was made as influential in moulding our beliefs are institutions formed
by rational beings acting in concert with one another.
Families, parties, nations, churches, brotherhoods, are
themselves rational institutions, and are the work of
rational creatures who were conscious of the bonds
which helped them to make themselves into a unity.
Every one of these organizations is constituted by
the efforts of the rational beings who realized them,
and any influence they exert on the individual is
really due to reason. We fearlessly assert that every
instance of the action of authority as opposed to rea-

son, set forth by Mr. Balfour, may be turned round and easily read as an instance of the influence of reason. We might take the case of language and by it illustrate the contention of Mr. Balfour.

Language moulds our feelings, emotions, desires, aspirations, beliefs, even our thoughts. Whatever he has said of authority may be said *a fortiori* on behalf of language. We are always under its influence; without its aid we could neither think adequately nor express our thought nor convey our thought to another. If we were to contrast language and reason as he has contrasted authority and reason, we could make a pretty effective contrast indeed. But then we should be at once told that we were engaged in an idle and unprofitable task, for language is itself the product of reason, and its influence is the influence of reason. That is our answer to Mr. Balfour; his antithesis between authority and reason is misleading, and it is irrelevant. The institutions which mould our lives, actions, and thoughts are themselves rational institutions, the products of that reason against which they are pitted by Mr. Balfour. Before he could make good the antithesis between reason and authority, he must do some work on both notions, he must first eliminate everything rational from the institutions he has named, and everything authoritative from reason, and when he has reduced the one to irrationality, and deprived the other of authority, then he may run the

o

antithesis as he pleases, and it will not be worth much.

There are elements in Mr. Balfour's book worthy of high praise, and there are conclusions with which I heartily agree, but to dwell on these at present is not my purpose. I found the argument of Mr. Kidd lying athwart my course, and I could not proceed until I got it out of my way. Mr. Balfour's work is so far coincident with that of Mr. Kidd; his antithesis between authority and reason is on all fours with the paradoxes of Mr. Kidd; and so far I have dealt with both. Perhaps the method common to both is even worse than the results to which they come. For the habit of setting part against part, and of straining the relation in which two or more elements in a larger unity stand to one another, until nothing but a relation of contradiction is left, is so fatal to all fruitful thinking, that I did not think the time wasted to show its falsity in the particular instances we have examined.

VII

PERSONALITY: ITS CHARACTER AND ITS MEANING

We have read the story which science has unfolded to us, and the wonder of the story has grown. We have come to see that the unity has grown greater and more complex, and the diversity tends ever more to unity. We have come to a unity greater than we can grasp. Not a fixed, static, unchanging unity, but one that grows, develops, becomes more and more, and yet maintains itself. Thus we came to the great organism of humanity—an organism made up of organisms, relatively independent of one another, but held together not by visible or physical bonds, but by bonds of another kind but not the less real. A unity made up of living unities, each of which is so far a self-contained whole, calls on us to widen our conceptions if we are to grasp the reality. Unities conscious of themselves, self-moved, self-guided, self-trained, in a measure, and held to the whole by bonds which can at any moment be broken; the thought of a unity composed of such makes us acquainted with a kind of force or power unknown before. So varied are the

195

bonds that hold the social order together, that every one of them in turn has been looked at as a relation of opposition to the others. Self-interest was regarded as irreconcilable with the universal interest, authority was pitted against reason, intelligence against belief, and yet no one of these could be dispensed with if the social organism were to hold together and to make progress. Reason and authority are needed, self-interest is as necessary as the interest of the whole, science is needed as much as religion, and religion as much as science; in fact, without any of these qualities and acquirements of humanity, which men are so prone to place in irreconcilable opposition, the social organism could not exist, at least could not exist in its well being. So out of the life of the social organism in its relations to its members and its environment have arisen the sciences, arts, intellectual, ethical, and religious systems, in action among us to-day, the histories of which make up so much of the recorded thoughts of men. As we look at these thoughts and systems we see them living, moving, growing, ever approximating to an ideal, which is partly given and partly won by patient thought and work. The conviction deepens with the ages that there is a thought greater than our thought, a system larger than we can yet grasp, and an ideal formed for man and not merely by man.

Up to the present, we have looked at the world

disclosed to us and unveiled to us by science merely as it unfolded itself to us, as it would appear to a spectator gazing at it from without. We looked at it mainly for the purpose of learning what the story of the world would disclose to us of the intelligence and purpose at work in it. We have found intelligence, purpose, life, at work in the world, and all on a scale almost passing our comprehension. But now the question rises, What do we really know of intelligence, purpose, life? We know of many works of intelligence, and of many kinds of life. We know that an intelligent system may be impressed on a system of mechanical causes, and these may be constrained to work out a purpose. Watches, clocks, electric machines, steam-engines, and all machines made by men are intelligible systems in which mechanical causes work out a purpose according to the design of the worker. Looking as a spectator we saw another kind of mechanism, a mechanism in which the skill of the designer was within the mechanism, and the purpose was wrought out not by impressing a plan on alien material, but by an immanent movement from within. The skill of the designer was within the organism, and the process was by growth. An organism we saw was greater than a mechanism. Still we learned that there were organisms and organisms. Growth was common to them all, but some grew, not knowing the aim and purpose of their growth, impelled onwards by impulses of which they were unconscious, drawn by desires which ruled them, and which they did not rule.

In the unfolding of life we came to the advent of a being who to a certain extent knew himself and his purpose, who could reach his purpose and attain his ends by bending the environment to his purpose. This being could form a purpose and invent means for its realization. Can we obtain a nearer view of the life, which we saw to be manifested in the sciences, philosophies, and religions of the world? It was the most wonderful of the wonderful things of the world disclosed to us by science, and we naturally desire to know it more intimately. For our conception of the life at work in the world must be largely determined by the knowledge we may attain of the life at work in the being who has made the sciences. Can we look at that being, not merely as spectators of his work and of his way of doing it, but can we get inside, and see him in the inward working of his very nature, and watch himself and his purposes in the making?

Happily we are at home in this world, too. We are ourselves, and we are able to look at ourselves from within, and are able to look at the other side of the world, which from one side has engaged our attention so long. The world has a subjective side, and we look at it now from that point of view. Here we may well begin with Hume, who has set the problems which since his time are the main problems of psychology, ethics, and metaphysics. "For my part, when I enter most intimately into what I call *myself*, I always stumble on some particular perception or other of heat or cold, light or shade, love or hatred, pain or pleasure. I never can catch *myself* at any time without a perception, and never can observe anything but the perception. When my perceptions are removed for any time, as by sound sleep, so long am I insensible of *myself*, and may truly be said not to exist. And were all my perceptions removed by death, and could I neither think, nor feel, nor see, nor love, nor hate, after the dissolution of my body, I should be entirely annihilated, nor do I conceive what is farther requisite to make me a perfect non-entity. If any one, upon serious and unprejudiced reflection, thinks he has a different notion of *himself*, I must confess I can reason no longer with him. All I can allow him is that he may be in the right as well as I, and that we are essentially different in this particular. He may, perhaps, perceive something simple and continued which he calls *himself*, though I am certain there is no such principle in me. But setting aside some metaphysicians of this kind, I may venture to affirm of the rest of mankind, that they are nothing but a bundle or collection of different perceptions, which succeed each other with an inconceivable rapidity, and are in a perpetual flux and movement. Our eyes cannot turn in their sockets without varying our perceptions.

Our thought is still more variable than our sight; and all our other senses and faculties contribute to this change; nor is there any single power of the soul which remains unalterably the same, perhaps for one moment. The mind is a kind of theatre, where several perceptions successively make their appearance; pass, repass, glide away, and mingle in an infinite variety of postures and situations. There is properly no simplicity in it at one time, nor *identity* in different; whatever natural propensity we may have to imagine that simplicity and identity, the comparison of the theatre must not mislead us. They are the successive perceptions only, that constitute the mind; nor have we the most distant notion of the place where these scenes are represented, nor of the material of which it is composed." Thus spoke Hume in his chapter on "Personal Identity" in his "Treatise on Human Nature," Part IV., Sect. VI. Again he says: " It is evident that the identity which we attribute to the human mind, however perfect we may imagine it to be, is not able to run the several different perceptions into one, and make them lose their characters of distinction and difference, which are essential to them. It is still true that every distinct perception which enters into the composition of the mind is a distinct existence, and is different and distinguishable and separable from every other perception, either contemporary or successive." And one more sentence, " What we call mind is nothing but a heap or bundle or collection of different perceptions united together by certain relations, and supposed, though falsely, to be endowed with a certain simplicity and identity."

The questions thus stated by Hume and the answers to them have appeared in almost all treatises on psychology which have been written since his time. His answers have in the main been the answers of the English school of psychology, and they are found almost in their naked simplicity in the works of the two Mills, in Bain, Huxley, and Spencer. He has also set the problem of the self for psychologists generally, and they toil at the problem in your country and in ours. One may read the incisive discussion of the problem in James's " Psychology," and in the able discussions of Dr. Ward, and in many others. I take from the discussions simply what I need.

The introspective glance cast by Hume into his own mind and its working is graphically described. "The mind is a kind of theatre where several perceptions successively make their appearance, pass, repass, glide away, and mingle in an infinite variety of postures and situations." True, we are satisfied for a time, and then we ask, What is the theatre, and for whom is the show? Hume rather anticipates the question, for he warns us that "the comparison of a theatre must not mislead us," and then goes on to say they are "the successive perceptions only that constitute the mind. " Having made use of the theatre and suggested a possible spectator, the theatre and the spectator are at once withdrawn, while the suggestion of them remains. As we continue to think of the matter, we come to the conclusion that we are in the presence of a unique kind of thing, which seems be at the same time knower and known, actor and spectator, a show and the spectator for whom the show is. The spectator and the gliding perceptions attracted our attention, and played the part of occupying our thought, until we forgot to ask the important question of the person who is aware of the movements of the gliding sensations. Then we found that Hume had left out one-half of the whole business, and that the half without the action of which there would have been no report.

The gliding perceptions come and go, but not unobserved or forgotten. They are not separate, unrelated, or unreferred. They are present to a consciousness which is also present to them. Hume's spectator is a convenient person in psychology, and fulfils a useful function. As a fact, he is brought in now and then, when some such functionary is indispensable. All of us postulate him at some point or other, and we usually fancy we are looking on from without at the consciousness of somebody else. As a matter of fact, the only consciousness I can ever hope to know is my own. I can interrogate my own consciousness ; I can compare it with what others tell me is within their consciousness, but really my perceptions are mine; I am the only being aware of them: their gliding, passing, and repassing are for me alone, and apart from my recognition of them they are unrecognized.

We have thus to amend Hume's description, ând say the mind is a theatre in which it is itself actor and spectator, and the perceptions do not constitute the mind, for they are not even perceptions until they are referred to the mind. To put it in more modern phrase, there is not only a series of states of consciousness, there is also a consciousness of these states, and this last is the element neglected by Hume and by his successors. It is quite true that we can never interview a blank self, or stand face to face with a consciousness devoid of contents; true, also, that the mind is always found in a particular state of consciousness, but it is equally true that it is found in every state, and it is distinct from any state, for it is the condition of the existence and recognition of them all. We are not to look for the mind as if it were a thing among other things, a sensation among sensations, or a perception among perceptions, or as the sum of a series of sensations, rather we are to look for mind as the universal condition of the possibility of all experience. As Hoffding says: "Conscious life has three characteristics: (1) change and contrast as condition of the individual elements entering consciousness; (2) preservation or reproduction of previously given elements, together with connection between these and the new element; (3) the inner unity of recognition."

There is the series and the awareness of the series, and neither of the two can be neglected in any adequate account of consciousness. Presentation, preservation, recognition, and the combination of them all into the unity of experience — this is the fact which must be accepted, and cannot be explained. The toil imposed on the followers of Hume by their attempt to build something, which might pass for mind, out of the separate elements of the series of states of consciousness casts the labours of Sisyphus altogether into the shade. To make ropes out of sand is an easy task in comparison. When Mr. Spencer reduces the beginnings of experience to nervous shocks, and endeavours to build up experience out of these, he appears to succeed, because he brings in surreptitiously the idea of unity of the nervous organism, which speedily becomes transformed into a unity of consciousness. In truth, the unity has been present in the shocks all along, only Mr. Spencer kept it hidden until he needed it, and brought it out at a certain stage, when it could no longer be kept back, and he made it appear as a newly manufactured article.

In fact, the two are inseparable, though we seem to attend only to one of them at a time. Consciousness may be fully occupied with the object on which attention is concentrated, and that to the exclusion of the thought of itself. I watched the helmsman on the great ship on which I once crossed the Atlantic. He had enough to do, for there was a considerable storm on hand. I saw him watch the waves with his hand on the helm, I saw the tension of his arms, the firm planting of the foot, the swaying of the body, and the tug of war as the helm met the waves, and all the time there was no recognition of the self as the centre to which all the coördinated movements of mind and body were referred. To me, the onlooker, what was visible were the skilful watching of the ever varying movements of wind, water, and ship, the skilful adaptation of the helm to these, and the strenuous work which he did. His description of his work would scarcely have a reference to his mental processes, while mine as descriptive of his work would be full of such terms as would describe his mental apprehension of the varying conditions and the adjustment of his action to meet them.

To the fact that the man is directly conscious of the object, and only conscious of himself as the subject when he directs attention that way, may be ascribed the plausibility of the account Hume has given of the process. When we attend to the process of seeing, we attend to what is seen and to the seeing of it. There is a double process, and it is little wonder that a plain man does take little interest in the workings of his own mind. What is present to every state of consciousness is not distinctive of any state. But even a plain man is aware that to the ordinary states of consciousness there is added a consciousness that they have come and gone. It is not a proper recognition of the fact to suppose that several perceptions being given, their collective consciousness is also given, for the awareness of the series is something not given in the series. In short, there is, we repeat, a series of states of consciousness and a consciousness of the states. Consciousness is the specific feature or condition of all mental states; not as something added to, apart from, or antecedent to mental states, but as that element which constitutes them as mental states. Feeling, knowing, acting, are conscious states, modes of consciousness, and consciousness is not the sum of these, but the condition of their existence. We may write of feeling, knowing, willing, as unconscious, if we please, but these are phrases which have no contents for consciousness.

Faculties are modes of consciousness, but consciousness is not a faculty. It is impossible to regard it as the outcome of unconscious forces, nor can it be deduced or derived from anything else; we must just accept it in its uniqueness as the explanation of everything that can be explained, itself unexplained. We have the happiness of knowing it from both sides, we know it from without, in the same way as we know other objects of science; and we know it from within, can surprise it in its working, and constrain it to disclose its secret and manifest its nature and its vocation. While we affirm that consciousness must be assumed, and while it cannot be derived nor resolved into something simpler, still the conditions of its exercise may be studied. As we know it in ourselves it has a beginning, a growth, and a history. Thrust into the midst of conditions not realized, slowly learning to find itself at home in the world, and gradually coming to the knowledge that there is an external order to which it is related, the self-conscious being, in intercourse with things, comes, so far, to the knowledge of self and of the world. The story may be taken for granted here, at least so far as to assume that the finite personality grows to the recognition of itself. It comes to distinguish between self and not-self. There is the self and there is the not-self. But this does not carry us very far. It would give only a very vague objectivity, without a definite content.

Consciousness emerges from this vague state when it recognizes that there are distinctions among its objects, relations in which these may be gathered up. One thing is related to another, and the relations run together, and in virtue of these, consciousness begins to find itself in an ordered world, and comes to know that its own principles are realized in the objects it finds around it. In virtue of its own rational nature it recognizes that it is in a rational universe. One remark is necessary here on two distinctions which are often used as if they were conterminous. One is the distinction between self and not-self, and the other is that between subject and object. These are by no means of equal extent and content. The boundaries of the first distinction are fixed and determined, the boundaries of the second are constantly changing. The one may be called an ontological distinction, for it relates to the distinction between two things, which in their distinction may be supposed to make up the whole sphere of being. The distinction between subject and object describes a mental function. The contents of the two are constantly changing. At one moment the object may be this table, with its shape, colour, its material, and the next moment the object may be the mental process which passed through the mind when the table was the object. The object may be either the things in the outer world, or it may be the states of consciousness by means of which we deal with the outer world. It may be the thing I seem to see, or it may be the vision through which I see it.

This remark is necessary, for a great deal of talk has come into existence about subject and object, and many inferences drawn from the contrast, such as that there cannot be an infinite consciousness, for a subject implies an object; and if the self is subject, it cannot, also, be object, and so on, all of which disappears when we remember that the distinction between subject and object is not an ontological distinction, but only the form under which consciousness takes place. They are relations within one experience.

Let us remember, also, that we are dealing here and in the first place with finite selves, each of which has had an individual history, a growth to consciousness; not with a self rational, and fully self-conscious from the beginning. As we wisely form our conception of a man from the fully developed man, thoroughly furnished in all that concerns humanity, so we take our ideal of consciousness, not from the process by which it came to itself, but from what it manifests when it is fully realized. It is not necessary for our purpose to dwell on the natural history of the individual, but we must lay stress on one thing. The conception of self, like all other conceptions, is one of gradual growth, and the time of its perfect realization is, for us, not yet. If you ask a child what its idea of the self is, the most likely answer will be a reference to the outward appearance. The body is regarded as the self, and most people, not trained in philosophy, if asked about the self, will look for it as if it were laid on a shelf, a thing among other things. They are so immersed in present experiences that they never ask for whom and whose is the experience? The conception of self is not given ready made, it grows, it is acquired.

P

While the experience of self is always present to every mind, the conception of the self as the subject of experience may never come to clear consciousness. There is a clearness and vividness in self-consciousness which puts all other things into antithesis with itself. There is an assertiveness about it which is unique. The world falls into two divisions for each of us, — there is myself, and there is the universe of other persons and things, — and this antithesis is of a kind that abides. Other people there may be, they also may think, they may have experiences of the same kind, but these experiences lack the vividness and impressiveness of my experience of myself, as a living, feeling, thinking being. It is in this real concrete life of feeling that selfhood acquires vividness and reality. Self-experience may be the only form which self-consciousness may assume. The self may be so absorbed in the process of experience, so lost in the feelings, desires, thoughts, which occupy it from moment to moment, that it may never reflect on itself, and never ask consciously what it is. It may remain on this level all through its earthly life. Absorbed in its objects, living out its experience of pleasure, engrossed in its pursuits, and interested in the success of its plans, it may never seek to reflect on its own nature or on the wonder implied in the most simple experience. We may be active, energetic, far-sighted, and wise to the uttermost, and yet we may have never given a single hour to the

thought of that self which has all these characteristics.

The mind may direct itself on either element of experience to the neglect of the other, it may focus its
attention on the subject or on the object. Self-consciousness may remain at the level of the simple experience of itself, or it may advance to a conception of
the self as the subject of all possible experience for
the self. In any case, a perfect self-consciousness is
implicit in every consciousness. It is possible for a
self to advance to the conception of itself as the subject of experience, which takes up all impressions,
rules them, binds them into a system, and makes them
parts in one consistent experience. In that case self-
consciousness would have attained its ideal, for it
would have reached the goal of self-knowledge and
self-control. The conception of a perfect self-consciousness consists in the fact that it is in possession of itself, and can set the bounds of its own
experience. Self-knowledge, self-reverence, self-control, in these, and not in its finitude or infinitude, lies
the conception of a perfect selfhood.

Here, then, is the fundamental element in the conception of personality, the highest conception which
we know. A person is one who has experience of
self, and may advance to the conception of self as
the subject of all possible experience, at least, of all
experience of that self. Having obtained this point
of view, we ought to go farther and regard the self

as subject of all possible knowledge, for knowledge is possible, because all the objects of knowledge are or may be brought into relation to the self. Objects out of all possible relation to the self are for that self non-existent. Apart from the questions raised by the theory of knowledge, we look at the ethical side of conception of the self, as it is of the highest significance. Psychology tells us that there is a self, the theory of knowledge affirms the worth of the self as the subject of knowledge for which all objects are, and ethics enables us to look at the self in the process of self-realization and self-determination. Ethically, the self is presented to our view as in the light of its own ideal, determining itself in certain directions and to certain ends. It has to choose its ideals and to realize them.

The distinction between psychology, theory of knowledge, and ethics is not absolute, for every problem has these three aspects, and all meet together in the problem of the self. How is the self to be realized and to come to its ideal? To answer this question would lead us very far, but the answer which concerns us now is mainly ethical. From this point of view all our science is to be looked at in its bearing on conduct, in its tendency to build up character, and to guide conduct. As knowledge lies in its reference to the self, so ethics has its significance as the intelligible means for the realization of the self, not in its mere selfhood, but as a member of a kingdom of selves, each of whom is a self which ought to be helped to realize its ideal. Take sympathy, for example, and look at it psychologically, it is a feeling which has in it pleasure or pain. We may analyze it into its elements and set forth its psychological meaning, but when psychology has done its work, ethics begins, and shows that by means of sympathy the self realizes that it is only one in a kingdom of selves, each one of whom has a right to count for one in the kingdom of good. The self learns to judge not from the feeling of pleasure and pain which he experiences, but he judges his actions by the good or harm they do to others.

As the reference to self is the unity of our knowledge and of our experience, in the ethical life a similar synthesis must take place. We must take care lest we pay too large a price for our intellectualism, and for our tendency to reduce all things to system. We must not lose hold of the concrete, living, throbbing, palpitating individual, with all his interesting experience, and substitute a cold series of abstractions in his place. Nor ought we to make the ethical life a thing of mere feeling. It is of the essence of a self-conscious being that he can look back on the changing, impulsive, fluctuating life of himself, submit it to his own review and to his own reflection, and seek to find the principle on which he has lived, and to gather it up into a rational whole. The self-conscious being who can and will, with insight, foresight, and deliberation, set himself to do this is on the way to be a person in the fullest sense of the word. He takes what is given to him, transforms it and himself into a larger whole, and in so doing he has realized himself and attained to personality. Personality for finite beings is a goal to be attained, not an inheritance they have received.

Individuality and personality are to be distinguished from each other. Individuality is given, personality is won. An animal has individuality, it has all the impulses and feelings which tend to self-preservation and race-preservation, and can maintain itself in the struggle for existence. Man is also a self in this lower meaning of the word. He has his appetites, desires, passions, impulses, which demand satisfaction, and urge him on to action. These exist in him, and rise in him as readily as in any animal. If allowed to have their way uncontrolled, in their total working they would constitute the man as they appear to constitute the animal. But they do not, at least they need not, constitute man. As a fact they do not so, for man can subdue his impulses, rule his passions, control his desires, and make them servants to a higher purpose. He can reflect on the phenomena which make up his manifold life, and look at them in their relation to a final and permanent good. Man may take a critical view of his sentient and impulsive life, subject it to a judicial review, choose which tendencies may be repressed, and which may be strengthened and encouraged, and thus become a moral personality. "Man goeth forth to his work and his labour until the evening." Man may review, he has the power to review the impulsive course of his past life, can criticise it, arrest its course, change and subdue the lower, animal, merely natural self, and make himself subject to a rational ideal, and so build up, out of the plastic material of sensibility, a stable moral self. Character in this sense does not belong to an animal. Its life seems to be a life of natural and immediate sensibility, unchecked by any glimmering of life as a whole. But for man there is a human task. All the natural tendencies to activity, all the surging elements of natural sensibility, all the clamant impulses of his nature, have to be looked at by the rational self, criticised, judged, appraised, their relative worth established in the judgment of the rational being who measures the good of life as a whole. The life of man is not a struggle of natural tendencies, he is the subject which feels all the promptings of passion and desire, but he is also the critic and judge of these, and it is as critic that he is master of his own destiny.

"He saw life steadily and saw it whole," is a saying the profundity of which grows on us the more we think of it. It was spoken only of one, it is ideally true of every rational self-conscious person. Not lost in mere individuality, not swept along like a thing by the stream of feeling and impulse, but master of himself and of his work, ruler of himself and of his impulses, having regard to the worth of life as a whole, and measuring every experience by its worth for the whole of life; this is something of the meaning of the saying. Much is given to us, but the given is the individuality out of which the personality is to be made. To man is given the material out of which the rational personality is to be realized. Much is given, — race endowments, all that heredity can convey, temperament, constitution, — in fact, it would be tedious to enumerate all that is given to the individual. Time, place, circumstances, racial conditions, the atmosphere of society, and many other things are given, but the character is not given, it is wrought out by the man himself. These are given that we may realize our personality. To other beings the law of their life is given; man has to subject himself to law, and to choose the highest law to which he will subject himself.

The rational being has thus a work to do. The several elements in the individual life, the antithesis into which they tend to fall, the seeming contradictions between the sensual and the rational, between the individual and society, and all the other divergencies which might be stated, are to be harmonized in the unity of the personal life. But this is only one part of self-realization. To unite the several elements of the individual life so that there will ensue a realized harmony is a great achievement; it is still greater to unite the several personal lives in a synthesis of a larger sort. The individual is particular, personality is universal. All humanity is potentially in every man. Each of us has to outgrow the individual, and to attain to somewhat of that personality which is the conciliation of the several individual lives.

"Be a person and respect others as persons." "Always use the humanity in thine own person and in the persons of others," never as a means, but always as an end, or as it is in Shakespeare, "To thine own self be true, and it must follow as the night the day, thou canst not then be false to any man." Each person an end in himself, with a right to demand from the universe the means for the realization of himself, and every person a law to himself in virtue of the realized rationality within himself, that is the ethical ideal set before us, alas! how far from being realized! Still in our best moments we feel that this is the right ideal for a man. To feel the oneness of the rational self with all other rational selves in the world, to know that just as far as we realize the rational ideal of humanity in ourselves, we are *ipso facto* brought into oneness with all others who bear the mark of personality. This oneness does not mean the obliteration of differences, it does not do away with that characteristic note of a man which makes him himself something distinct from all other in the world, but it gives a place to him in the common kingdom, which is constituted by such a union of all as is consistent with the freedom of each. Our study of the personality of man leads to this conclusion, that personality is not to be suppressed, not to be submerged in a larger whole which will swallow it up as the river swallows up the snowflakes which fall on it; rather whatever the synthesis may be, it at least must be of a kind which will leave the person free to continue in his self-conscious activity, as a being that has worth and significance in himself. That is to say, that the larger unity of which we are in search must be constituted on another basis, and after another sort than any we have met in the course of our exploration. The cells which we came to know in their differentiated state as parts of one organism had a union among themselves only on condition that they were in subordination to the whole. They no longer maintained a separate existence. But the persons who make up a society maintain their relative independence; there are characteristics which they cannot give up if they are to remain persons. They must continue to exert all the modes of their consciousness, must live out their own feeling, thinking, acting, and, in a word, they must be themselves and not others. In this continuance of their personal life and growth consists their worth for society, and their worth in themselves. Not to be ground in a social mill until all angularities are rubbed off: no, that is not the ideal; rather the ideal is to sharpen the angularities and keep them in all their picturesqueness, so that there may be the fullest development of the uniqueness of every personality, along with the fulness of the rational unity constituted by a spiritual integration of such personalities.

Such a unity can only be constituted by the rational choice of such personalities. The unity of a barrel is made by the hoops, the unity of an organism is constituted by a principle of life acting from within, the unity of a social organism must be constituted by the self-surrender of the members to the whole, and of the whole to the members. Such a unity is not yet, but it is coming nearer. At all events, we have made such progress as to be able to set forth in some adequate way the conditions of such a social union. We can see that the ways of holding peoples and nations together which have prevailed through the past have not been ideal ways. Standing armies, brute force, repressive legislation, one people holding another in subjection, — these are not ideal ways of reaching social union. But on these I am not called to dwell. What I am concerned with is the necessary condition to any social union, namely, that there must be full scope in it for the development of the individual to a personality, and that the surrender of the person to the good of the society must be deliberate, rational, free, in a word, it must be rational self-surrender.

The spirit of the society may pass into the members of that society, and the social ethos be realized in each member, but it will be realized by him in his own characteristic way. Character may be as distinctive as faces are, the common type is there, but each face has something distinctive. So with the personality, it is one, but with distinctions. For this spiritual thing which we call personality is the most unique product of time. Imperfectly realized as it is, it yet presents us with the most complete type we know of imperviousness, and resistance to all merely external influences. Force may be brought to bear upon it, it may be crushed out of visible existence, you may cage it, imprison it, and the caged imprisoned thing may sing, "My mind to me a kingdom is." It may maintain its sturdy independence, and if it is to be subdued, it must be by influence of another kind. If it is to recognize itself as a member of a larger unity, that unity must come to it in a fashion which will recognize the worth of the person. There are limits to the demands which the social organism may make. None can have the right to demand from a person the surrender of that which would make him cease to be a person and which would turn him into a thing.

These remarks have a wide significance, which is not limited to the discussion of social questions, on which I do not enter. They have a bearing on philosophical and ethical questions, the discussion of

which is occupying the attention of the deepest
thinkers on this side and on our side of the water.
These questions will be looked at later. Meanwhile
let us look at the process by which the rational being
may be persuaded to serve, obey, love, and work in
union with his fellows. For by persuasion alone can
this result be rightly wrought out. It is by ideals
that the rational man is led to self-surrender. It is
by an appeal to his rational nature that the process
of self-realization can be guided to its destined end.
Each aspect of our complex nature makes its own
contribution to the ideal. Nor can science make any
progress without an appeal to an ideal. From the
experience that the self has of the energy it exerts
in its own action, science leaps forth to the conception
of an infinite and eternal energy from which all
things proceed. From the intelligent action of the
self and the room for that action which it experiences in the world, science obtains the conception of
an intelligence which is equal to the ordering of the
world. Reason is postulated as the cause of the
rationality of the world. From the appreciation of
beauty and harmony which man finds in the world,
the æsthetic ideal of an infinite source of beauty is
constructed. The conscience of man thirsting after
righteousness cannot rest until it reaches an ideal of
perfect righteousness in which there is no becoming,
and the heart of man demands an ideal of perfect
goodness and love. As long as any demand of

intelligence, conscience, heart, or reason is unrecognized, there can be no peace for man.   Only when all the claims of the many-sided nature of man are recognized in the conception of an all-wise, holy, loving, all-powerful God, can man realize himself.

Are these ideals real?   Are they not the objectification of our own needs?   Are they the Brocken shadows of ourselves cast upon the wastes of space?   Does not the idea of an infinite personality land us in contradiction?   Well, I do not hesitate to say that for the interpretation of our experience, we are entitled to make those assumptions without which experience is not possible.   This is axiomatic.   In fact, it is done by every one who ventures to make universal propositions.   Every one assumes in his philosophy that, to use the words of Mr. Spencer, "I am in the presence of an infinite and eternal energy from which all things proceed."   We are entitled to ask, whence this conception has come?   For it is certain that our finite experience, considered in itself, cannot make such an affirmation.   As merely quantitative, we cannot measure, weigh, or reckon an infinite.   We reach the idea of infinite power by recognizing that we cannot set any limit to it, yet our positive notion of power is derived from our own activity.   If we grant to Mr. Spencer the conception of infinite and eternal energy, we still maintain that the notion is positive, not negative. Infinite and eternal are not negative, they merely set forth that there are objects to the worth and excellence of which we can set no limits.

The main object of these remarks is to show the inconsistency of those who first make universal propositions themselves, and refuse to others the same right. If we can form an idea of power, if we can without contradiction speak of an infinite and eternal energy, we have opened up the way to the affirmation of other ideals. The affirmation of an energy is the raising of one part of our experience to its ideal, and the idea of force has no better inherent right to be thus raised to the infinite than any other idea has. But a great many raise this conception to an ideal height, and then use it to criticise all other ideals. If we speak of perfect righteousness, of infinite intelligence, of perfect beauty, or of eternal goodness and love, we are at once told that we are anthropomorphic, and those who say so forget that the notion of energy is quite as anthropomorphic as any of these mentioned. In truth, the contention, if carried out consistently, would destroy science altogether, and limit our thought to what happens in our own time and within the narrow circle of our purely personal experience, and that in the narrowest sense of the word "experience." If, as the correlative of our experience of power, Spencer can speak of an infinite and eternal energy, he may not limit the rights of others. If infinite power is involved in our experience of finite power, then with a right as good infinite reason is involved in the exercise of the finite reason we know, aye, and with a much better claim. Perfect righteousness, holiness free from all imperfection, goodness, and love are involved in the finite experience of the righteousness, holiness, and love realized among men. I know no reason why they claim reality for their ideal, and refuse reality to mine. I am in relation to an external world which reveals itself to me through my senses, and I can interpret these manifestations into a system. If my experience thus interpreted is justified by the result, as it is, is the objective reference exhausted by this interpretation of sense experience? Have we not acted on the supposition that all our experience must have an objective reference? In my intellectual action I must think there is an intelligible world, in my moral action I make the same assumption, namely, that heart and conscience in me are related to an objective authority which has a right to guide my life and dictate my action.

These ideals stand on the same level, or, if there is any preference, the preference is in favour of these ideals prescribed by the necessities of the higher nature of man. But I do not pitch them against each other. For we need for our thought and for our life the conception of the infinite and eternal energy, and we go on to say that this energy is, also, the realization of all ideals, and all these ideals are realized in the One Eternal energy from which all things proceed and to which they all tend to return. The theistic belief is that all these positive ideals are realized in one infinite personality to whom we are related in many ways, whom we may know, and who may make Himself known to us. Now the only category we know in which and by means of which we may set forth the infinite qualities of such a being is just that of personality. It is the widest word known to us and the greatest unity. Even in the finite person, how many qualities meet! Mind and body, matter and spirit, instinct and reason, feeling, thought, and action, consciousness of pleasure and pain, of good and evil, all brought together within the synthesis of one experience. We say then, if we have the right of raising any part of our experience to its ideal, *a fortiori* we have the right to raise the whole synthetic unity to its ideal, and that gives us the conception of a perfect personality.

But personality is a limitation, and how can you ascribe a limitation to the unlimited ? We hear this urged by many in our land, indeed, it is the favourite agnostic position. It has been often argued during the last half century, and I shall not spend much time on it. With Lotze, I would say that perfect personality can only be found in the infinite. The ideal personality is one in which there is no becoming, no limits save those set by itself, which is in perfect possession of itself, and sets the bounds of its own experience and determines all its states. To the reality

of such a personality we are led by all the experience
of man. It is the demand of the reason, the postulate of our moral nature, the claim of the will, which
requires it as the guarantee of its venture of faith,
launched as it is on a world not realized. To me the
difficulty is not whether personality should be predicated of God, but whether so great a word should be
a predicate of man. At the best, we are imperfect
persons, with a personality not realized, dependent,
having our states and our experience largely set for
us, not by us, not able to determine wholly either the
character or the limits of our experience. Yet the
personality in ourselves is so far given as to enable
us to see what a perfect personality is.

In fact, I would sum up the whole argument in this
one word, "personality." I do not employ the word
"self-consciousness," as some do, for it seems to me
that self-consciousness is only one element of personality. It is simply the outline of personality which has
to be filled up with the elements of concrete experience
to redeem it from mere abstractness. Reason, intelligence, righteousness, love, are mere metaphors when
divorced from their significance as qualities of a person. This is the conclusion to which we are led by
the history of science and philosophy, and, as we shall
see, this is the supreme demand of religion, and if it
is not conceded, religion is impossible in any true
sense of the word.

VIII

RELIGION: ITS NATURE, HISTORY, AND DEMANDS

In speaking of religion, there are two propositions I desire to make regarding it at the outset. The first is that religion is universal and belongs to man as man. All men have been conscious of their dependence on a power greater than themselves, and have felt a necessity of being on good terms with that power. They have believed in the existence of such a power; they have sought to propitiate that power in many ways; and they have recognized that that power had prescribed for them a certain kind of life. The result of investigation leads to the historical conclusion that there has been no people without a religion; at least, such a people has not yet been discovered. A religion gives a creed to believe, commands to obey, and consolations to be enjoyed. And these are elements in every religion.

A second proposition I venture to make is that religion is universal in another aspect; namely, it belongs to every part of human nature. It is not a matter merely of the reason, nor is it merely based on feeling, nor is it only directed toward action. It appeals to the whole consciousness of man, and to every mode of it. It is rational, emotional, and volitional. It gives truth for the intelligence, consolations for the heart, motive and guidance for the will. It is necessary to insist on these commonplaces, for religion has been identified with philosophy, and the problem of the one has been stated as if it were the problem of the other; it has been denuded of every rational element and transformed into a mere matter of feeling; and it has been identified with ethics, and its commands made to be simply ethical injunctions. Now my contention is that religion is a philosophy. It has truth to proclaim, but it is more. Religion is emotional; it addresses the emotions, quickens the affections, and purifies the heart, but it is more. It does command and prescribe a certain kind of life, but it does more. In fact, religion is at home within the whole complex nature of man, and makes its appeal to the whole man, and insists on being with him in all his thinking, feeling, acting.

Thus addressing the whole man, and thus interested in all his activity, it follows that no effort and no work of man is indifferent to his religion. It is sometimes said that there is a conflict between religion and science, between religion and philosophy, but such a conflict is not necessary nor is it reasonable. It might as well be said that there is a conflict between religion and commerce, between religion and architecture, and between religion and any other form of human activity. No doubt such conflicts have been, and books have been written to set forth the history of the conflict between science and religion, between philosophy and religion, just as books have been written to describe conflicts between different forms of religion. It seems to me that such conflicts are unnecessary; and it would be well to say broadly that religion has its rights, and these have to be recognized in any thoughtful treatment of human life, thought, and history. It is happily not necessary to insist on this nowadays, when every statement as to the phenomena of religion in any part of the world and from any age of history is eagerly welcomed, and forms material for serious study to the most thoughtful of living men. They eagerly investigate the phenomena of religion, if from no other interest, at least from the point of view that here are real beliefs of men, and it is important for men to know and understand them. Thus the activity of thought in this department is immense, and books by the dozen issue from the press dealing with the philosophy of religion, the making of religion, the history of religions, and so on. We cannot complain of a want of interest in this great question, even though we may complain of the inadequate account given of the origin, the nature, and the truth of religion.

Of religious belief Mr. Spencer says truly, "Thus the universality of religious ideas, their independent evolution among different primitive races, and their great vitality unite in showing that their source must be deep-seated instead of superficial. In other words, we are obliged to admit that if not supernaturally derived as the majority contend, they must be derived out of human experiences, slowly accumulated and organized." ("First Principles," pp. 14–15.) Again, " Considering all faculties, as we must do on this supposition, to result from accumulated modifications caused by the intercourse of the organism with its environment, we are obliged to admit that there exist in the environment certain phenomena or conditions which have determined the growth of the feeling in question, and so are obliged to admit that it is as normal as any other faculty." (P. 16.) When we ask what is the function of this faculty, admitted by Mr. Spencer to be as normal as any other, we find on examination of his voluminous works that it has scarcely any function at all. It has the strange peculiarity, surely very strange for a normal faculty, of always being in the wrong, of taking illusions for realities, and of reaching wrong conclusions during all the years of its operation. Mr. Spencer assigns all that is knowable to science, and leaves to religion all that transcends knowledge, with the assurance that let religion strive as it may, it can never reach reality, and never attain to knowledge. It seems rather hard to treat at the outset all the religious strivings of religion as without a goal or a legitimate result, and all the religious experience of mankind as vain. Yet this is what Mr. Spencer does, he leaves to religion its mystery, but he leaves it nothing else. Still, let us take his admission that the religious faculty is as normal as any other faculty, and that there are conditions and phenomena in the environment corresponding to man's religious nature. With this concession we may take our own way of ascertaining what in the environment corresponds to the religious needs of man, and what man has discovered that feature of the environment to be.

We take with us the presupposition that there is a correspondence between experience and reality, that as room has been found in the world for human activity, that as methods corresponding to the rational methods of human reason are found at work in the world, and as man has found his mathematics and his logic at work in the world, so this great part of human experience which we call religion has its sphere and function, its place and its truth, in the universe in which man has found himself. There is no reason why religion should be limited to what transcends knowledge, or why its function should be to deal only with the unknowable. We submit that a philosophy which aspires to be perfectly unified knowledge, fails if it does not deal with religious experience, or take into account the action of this faculty admitted to be normal. In fact, philosophy, in all the forms and phases of it in vogue at the present hour, admits the obligation, though it must be said it discharges the function most imperfectly. Religion is for it a special form of the philosophical problem as their system sets it forth. For the Hegelian idealist, it is only the last and highest form of the philosophical thesis; for the positivist, it is only a kind of after thought added by the founder to make room for a new experience of his own. For the agnostic, religion represents, so far as it has ideas, the necessary failure which comes to man when he tries to formulate his notions of what transcends knowledge. Thus, while philosophy seeks to have its philosophy of religion for the most part, the religion seems to escape, and the philosophy alone remains.

It is not my purpose to dwell on the history of religion, nor on the various modes of its manifestation; nor do I mean to set forth, still less to criticise, the various theories of the origin, nature, and function of religion in vogue at the present hour; nor shall I spend my time endeavouring to set forth a philosophy of religion. Any of these would be a worthy work, were there time for it. What is sought to be done in this lecture is, simply, the sequel of what has been attempted up till now. We say that as the thought of man has widened he has been constrained to recognize the existence of wider and wider unities in the synthesis of his knowledge in relation to reality.

From physical unities held together by pressure, to organic unity of the organism, to the higher unity of life, to the unity of personal life, to the spiritual unity of the social organism, we found ourselves bound to rise, and we felt that each higher unity made a larger demand on our power of conception. We felt tempted at every upward turn of the spiral to substitute for the concrete reality some easier conception, something more easily grasped and handled. Yet we found that these higher unities were rational unities constituted, perhaps, by a higher reason than ours; and we ought to treat them as the goal of our thinking. Purposely, these higher unities were looked at from various points of view, and the question of religion was omitted from the treatment, lest it would complicate it unduly. Of course, religion was an all-important factor in personal and social experience from the beginning, and the higher unities could not have been constituted apart from it. But the consideration of religion widens the problem immeasurably. It brings with it an eternal element, it widens the horizon of the present by bringing into our life the relations in which we stand not only to our fellow-men, but the relations in which we stand to God. It widens the boundaries of the past, for it compels us to think of the human beings who have lived and died, as living at this hour, and of all the dead as contemporaries, all existing somehow in the eternal present. It casts our thoughts forward to the future, and compels us to face not only the problems of the present life, but to face them with the added burden of the bearing they have on the eternal future of ourselves and others.

Thus religion by its thought of God and immortality widens our horizon immeasurably, and transforms every scientific and philosophic problem into a problem of much wider significance. It therefore needs larger resources for adequate dealing with its special problems than are needed by science and philosophy. It needs a deeper than philosophic faith, a wider than scientific experiment. For from the nature of the case many of its beliefs cannot be subjected to scientific verification. None of us know yet what it is to die, and none of us have experience of what comes after death; and so the beliefs, the ineradicable belief in the life which follows after death, must be based on hope, or on our belief in the testimony of one who knows. The belief in immortality has been one of the most persistent beliefs of men, and it has all the marks of a rational belief worthy of a rational being; but from the nature of the case it cannot be verified in the way in which I have verified for myself the existence of New York. We may expect to verify it by and by, but the time is not yet.

If the fact corresponds to the belief, if all who have lived somewhere in the eternal present, if Moses, Isaiah, Socrates, Plato, if the great thinkers, prophets, poets, religious guides and leaders of the human race are living at this hour, surely that widens our thought of the unity of men, more specially if we believe, as we must, that they are still in some sort of relation to us and we to them. It shows to us that religion with its characteristic beliefs brings into the problem elements which philosophy laid little stress on, which indeed it has for the most part neglected. The environment for religious people becomes much wider and deeper. It is not for religion what it is for philosophy, — the concourse of people living at the present hour, with all the inherited influences, transmitted tendencies, and accumulated thought and experience of the past; it means also that these living forces are still living, and all the people of the past may become the living environment of the present for any one of us. If religion has this as a living belief, it must exercise a corresponding influence on life and conduct. And this belief widens the problem of religion beyond the range of philosophy. It becomes the highest problem that man can grapple with, for it has brought with it elements which have not been prominent in the treatment which philosophy bestows on its problems.

Religion teaches us to look at the social environment from a new point of view. We saw the significance of the family, the city, the state, and other institutions in the training of men. We see, also, that heredity does not exhaust the debt we owe to our ancestors, nor have their gifts to us descended altogether by the line of direct descent. Men have lived, wrought, felt, acted, and they have written their experience, and the written thoughts and deeds of former thinkers and workers have become the most effective means of training their successors. This is a commonplace. But the commonplace is transfigured when religion grasps it, and gives it the colour of its own faith and hope. It tells us that no one of the achievements done by men in the past is lost, nor are they lost who did them. The men who opened out paths into strange countries of thought and experience, who widened the bounds of knowledge, and left us examples of what human life and thought may be, are not passed into oblivion and non-existence, they are somewhere and doing some worthy work to-day. Assume this hope to have a true ground, and we add immeasurably to the worth of human life and endeavour. Life assumes a new meaning, hope takes a grander sweep, and the horizon is widened beyond measure. It is the characteristic way of religion thus to introduce grandeur into our thoughts, and a deeper worth into our estimate of things.

It is the mark of religion, in particular, to introduce the note of eternity into our estimate of the most common of our experiences. Philosophy takes note in its own way of eternity, but it grasps it with a faltering hand, and follows the clew with a hesitating foot. But religion neither falters nor hesitates, but boldly places all the objects of its contemplation in the light of eternity. In particular, it places persons in this light, looks at them as beings who shall live forever, and regards all actions, feelings, and thoughts as something which has a significance that will never die. Above all the note of religion in its estimate of men is that it looks at this life and this world as the place for the making of persons, for the building up of character, and for the preparation of them for a place and a work in the kingdom of God. Philosophy at its best does not attempt so high a flight. It takes shorter views. Evolutionary philosophy limits its view to the lifetime of the sun, or, if it takes a longer view, it contemplates a collision with some other solar system, which will scatter the material of both systems into a cosmic cloud, and from such a nebula a process of evolution may again emerge to run a similar course. It contemplates with as much composure as is possible to it the wreck of all the toil and labour of the world. All the thoughts and work of men, even that thought which evolved the theory, vanish and leave not a wreck behind. Even Hegelian evolution, which is a greater and higher thing than Darwinism, leaves us without a future, and its outlook is bounded by the life that now is. Indeed, the highest product of evolution in the hands of Hegel seems to be a Prussian at the beginning of the present century — a respectable product of evolution certainly, but one that does not seem to have exhausted the resources of civilization.

Where philosophy falters, and where it almost

fears to tread, religion boldly enters in and makes a home for itself. In virtue of this assured hope, which it may be said has been ever a characteristic of religion in every form of it, religion has transformed the problem of life, and made it a greater problem than ever. It has given to man a new environment, by the very fact that it has placed him in eternity. It has given a new meaning to our endeavour by showing that all we do has a meaning that time cannot exhaust. If I learn to look at the man in the street as a man who shall live forever, then I dare not use him as a means for any end of mine. I dare not attenuate him to an aspect as I find myself in constant danger of doing, for he has in him the eternal worth of personality. Philosophy may teach us of the worth of man, it may tell me that as a person I must treat others as persons, and always use the humanity in my own person and in the persons of others as an end and never as a means; but religion gives a new sanction to this teaching when it tells me of the worth of a person as a being of eternity. If the consequences of actions are exhausted here, if the building up of character has a meaning only within time, if the work we can do can live only in the memory of our successors, then clearly the motives which have only this temporal sanction are of less strength than those that religion enforces with its doctrine of immortality.

As the advent of reason has transfigured all the

feelings, emotions, desires, thoughts, and volitions of the rational being, so a further transfiguration takes place in the plastic hand of religion. We may not speak of the advent of religion as if the appearance of it was subsequent to that of rationality, for man has always been a religious being. But religion does transfigure every aspect of the human being, gives a new character to his affections, a new stimulus to his action, a new motive to his endeavour, and a new aim to his aspiration. It brings new light to his intelligence, and a new strength to his will. Only one of the great thoughts of religion has been yet looked at by us, but how great has been the significance of this thought for man! The hope of immortality has had a larger influence than can be traced here, but let what has been indicated suffice for the present.

The particular forms in which this hope has embodied itself are as various as are the races of men. It is quite true that these embodiments of the hope of the future life have not been of an elevating or of a purifying kind. True that the peoples thought of the future life in colours borrowed from the scenery, the occupations, the vicissitudes of the present life. The happy hunting ground of the Indian, the perpetual battle of Valhalla, the happy halls of the Egyptian, and all the innumerable forms which have been drawn by the imaginations of men to set forth the conditions of the future life, do not convey to us any real conception of what that life may be. In truth, we are not able to picture to ourselves what life in these new conditions may be, while we may be fully persuaded of the reality of that life, and the belief of it may have the largest and most beneficial influence on our conduct. It is quite legitimate for us to take our conception of the future life from the highest and best thought of it, set forth in the highest form of religion known to man, and to use all the other forms of it simply as testimonies to the universality and influence of that belief. Life and immortality have been brought to light, and these are the sure possession of the highest religion at this present hour.

The belief in immortality and the belief in a divine being or beings have always gone together. There is no tribe without its God, as there is none without a religion. At all events, every tribe which has come within our knowledge had a belief in beings or a being superior to himself, whom he had to please and to propitiate, and on whose favour he depended for any good he desired. It is true that the forms in which he pictured this superior being vary widely. Almost all things on earth, under the earth, and over the earth, every phenomenon on land or sea or sky has been taken as a symbol or sign of the divine. The spirit worshipped, feared, and served may have had its home in the sun, moon, or stars, on the mountains or the plains, may have dwelt in anointed stones or sculptured pillar, in fact, there is nothing which may not be or become a dwelling place of the spirit in which man believed. Anything might assume a sacred form, and attain to a sanctity arising from some relation to the divine being. Thus there were sacred stones, sacred trees, sacred groves, as well as sacred places, persons, and sacred guilds. So also there is no form of service which has not had a place in the observances which men have devoted to the worship of the divine beings in whom men believed. The sacred rites were innumerable, and the sacrifices offered included all that a man had to give, — goods, possessions, cattle, slaves, children, wife, even personal honour and life itself were offered, if in no other way the lost fellowship could be restored. Thus the belief in a superior being receives illustration from all the religious experience of the race. The intensity of the belief, and the reality of it, are attested by the earnestness and thoroughness of their religious service. It was a belief that influenced conduct in the most practical way. It was no half-hearted belief, it was living and real.

Whether we regard religious belief as rational and one that is in correspondence with reality, or whether we regard it as superstitious and unjustified, there can be no difference of opinion as to the reality and intensity of it, and the powerful influence it has exerted on the thoughts and lives of men. Whether true or false, the belief in a divine being is a sign of the greatness of man. It reveals a power in man whereby he is enabled to transcend the present and the visible, to pierce through the veil of sense and time, and to think of himself as related to an unseen power to whom he could assign no limits. How earnestly he strove to find God, how eagerly he sought to serve Him, let the records of the religions of the world testify. Happily the labours of our numerous scientific workers in anthropology have made us acquainted with the forms which religion has assumed among the peoples of the earth. No doubt the facts are given to us mostly as illustrations of a theory, but still the facts are there, and we may separate them from the theory. One arranges the facts to set forth the theory that ancestor-worship is the root of every religion, another finds in animism the first outline of religion, and traces its development upwards through polytheism to theism. While others start with the worship of nature and natural phenomena, and then strive to find a method of development which will give the phenomena of the higher religions. The important thing for us is, not the various theories, but the universal fact they all assume. These theories I do not criticise here.

This, however, must be said, that no theory has as yet commanded general assent. The ghost theory accounts for very few of the facts, and the theory of Tylor is met by the array of facts gathered together by Mr. Andrew Lang, and these facts cannot be explained on the animistic view. How did savage tribes come to believe in a God, of great power, of an ethical character, and of great and high attributes, when all their other beliefs were on the rudest savage level? That such is the case is abundantly proved by Mr. Lang, and also by your own Dr. Brinton. To these writers and to many others I refer for the proof of this statement, as my space is very limited. "Our next step," says Mr. Lang, retracing the steps of his argument, "was to examine in detail several religions of the most remote and backward races, of races least contaminated with Christian or Islamite teaching. Our evidence, when possible, was derived from ancient and secret tribal mysteries and sacred native hymns. We found a relatively Supreme Being, a Creator, sanctioning morality, and unpropitiated by sacrifice, among peoples who go in dread of ghosts and wizards, but do not always worship ancestors. We showed that the anthropological theory of the evolution of God out of ghosts in no way explains the facts in the savage conception of a Supreme Being." ("The Making of Religion," pp. 327-8.)

The evidence attainable as to the belief in God among early men, goes to prove that, be the source of that belief what it may, they did believe in a powerful, moral, eternal, omniscient Father and Judge of men. Religion and morality were not disjoined, they were united, and served the same end. "We see that even in its rudest forms religion was a moral force; the powers that man reveres were the side of social order and tribal law; and the fear of the gods was a motive to enforce the laws of society, which were also the laws of morality." (Robertson Smith, "Religion of the Semites," p. 53.) Religion in alliance with ethics, moral conduct enforced by the commands of the Supreme Being, this is presented to us in the evidence gathered even by Spencer in his "Sociology." It is to be admitted that the conclusion is not universal, that religion is often divorced from morality, and rites and ceremonies have often ceased to have a moral reference. It is a fact that meets us in the history of advancing peoples that their religion remains conservative, while their intelligence, their morality, and their civilization makes progress. This conflict is often symbolized in the fact that there is a change in the character and names of the gods of a people. A change of the mind of the people may have left no trace save in a revolution among the gods. When Varuna ceased to be the chief figure among the Aryan gods, and Indra took his place; when Ahura Mazda ceased to occupy the highest place in the thought of Iran, and attention was concentrated on Mithra, —the change indicated a profound revolution in the mind of the worshippers, and a change from a higher to a lower ethical platform.

In truth, part of the tragedy of the ages lies in

the fact that religion tends to be conservative, while knowledge has grown ; the very sacredness of religion makes it averse to change. Thus a religion and the gods it worships may no longer fitly serve the higher needs of an advancing people. And religion may become hostile to morality. The rules it sanctioned fit for one stage of culture may be seen to be quite unsuitable for a higher stage. It is well illustrated in the case of Greece, Rome, and in fact in all the progressive nations of antiquity, in which we find elaborate explanations of the myths of the gods, and allegorical meanings are found for the stories of the adventures of the gods which had become incredible, as well as revolting. Thus the mind of the more educated was led away from religion ; and while the rites and ceremonies were duly observed, the feeling these represented had passed away. It is to be acknowledged that there have been religions which were irrational, childish, and immoral, and the con-ception of God contained in them was altogether unworthy. That is only to say that religious concep-tions were on a level with all the other conceptions in the savage mind at that stage of culture. But there has been a process by means of which religion has established its claim on man, and has absorbed all that is best and truest in his being, commending it-self to his whole nature, to his conscience, his heart, and his reason as the most precious endowment of his life. There has also been a progressive purification of the idea of God till God becomes the moral ideal, and the Object of reverent worship.

It has been a long process, and it is a process which will task the powers of man for ages yet to come. As we look back on the progress of religion, we see by no means a regular and orderly development. We see in some cases that the idea of the divine had scarcely in it any worthy element. The gods were often thought to be almost non-moral, capricious, selfish, lustful, hateful, and impure. Yes, and even when the moral sense revolted against the kind of action represented as divine, reverence constrained silence. For a time the sense of dependence and the feeling of awe constrain to silence, and the commands of the god continue to be obeyed until the moral nature, gathering strength and courage, rises in revolt, and the relation between religion and morals becomes very strained. Sometimes, in such a crisis, many things may happen. Morality may go one way and religion another, or there may be a reformation of the religion, and a conception of God and His character may arise more fit and adequate to meet the higher thoughts of the worshipper, or there may be a new religion introduced under the impulse of a great religious leader. Examples of each may readily be found in the history of religion. The beginning of morality may be found in a criticism of the prevalent religion of the hour. Anaxagoras, in the history of Greek thought, began the criticism of the religious teaching embodied in the poems of Homer and Hesiod, Xenophanes carried on the same necessary work, and Plato from a higher platform set himself to purify the religious conceptions of his time. Plato's criticism was not altogether destructive, rather it was an endeavour to remove from the character of the divine every trace of immorality, and to set forth the character of God as righteous, true, and good. The history of the strenuous attempts of the peoples to reach some worthy conception of the unseen power on whom they felt they depended, cannot be given here. It is a long and a painful story.

It may, however, be said that we do find in the history of almost every people times when there is a conflict between the religion and the moral elements of character they had come to reverence and observe. Sometimes, too, the conflict arises because the claims of religion are in advance of the moral power of obedience, and the ethical character of their god is far above their thought and their desires. Not often do we find a correspondence between the morality and religion of the people. In a progressive people the morality outgrows the religion, in a people given over to self-indulgence the religion is higher than the morality. Only once in history do I find that a progressive development of morals was also a progressive revelation of the character of God. There in Israel the apprehension of the character of

God was the signal of moral progress. The religious and the moral consciousness of that people was bound in a real unity, just because God was an ethical God.

What has been said amounts to this, that the religious needs of mankind were deep, wide, and abiding, and that satisfaction for these needs was difficult of attainment. When the people had a conception of a creator, ethical and powerful, it often happened that they were not able to use that thought for the practical guidance and consolation of their life. Either the thought made too great a demand on them, or they thought that God had no need of them and their service, or they were attracted by spiritual beings nearer to them who demanded service, so we find that among many tribes the worship of the creator God fell into the background, and the thought of Him had no practical effect on them. Still the thought and the fact were there, ready for use when the need for such a thought arose.

The religious history of mankind is, without doubt, a record of high and lofty endeavour, begun ever anew after many a disastrous failure, and carried on with the hope that man will one day attain to the knowledge of God, the knowledge of whom is eternal life. Men have held fast to the belief in a supreme power, even when they had found no worthy thought by which they might think of Him. The divorce between religion and morality, the reverence which made them slow to change the traditional thought of the unseen power whom their fathers believed in, the passionate seeking after a true thought of God which drove them at last into open rebellion and revolt against an unworthy and untrue religion, are elements in that age-long striving after God which assuredly would never have been perpetuated throughout the generations were there no God to seek. It is also true that these perturbations of spirit, these dissatisfactions with the teaching of almost all religions, are simply testimonies to the belief that God must be a worthy God when they have found Him. Every criticism of religion, rightly viewed, is really a protest against an unworthy or inadequate representation of the divine. God must be the ideal in whom all ideals meet. In Him must be the ideal of power, for from Him all power, as known to man, must flow. In Him is the ideal of reason, intelligence, wisdom; for all the arrangements of the universe are His appointments. Nothing exists beyond His power, nothing hidden from His omniscience. Then He has a purpose and a meaning in all His working, and He knows what His purpose is. He is righteous, just, holy, good, the ruler of the nations, and the judge of all.

These characteristics of God are drawn from ancient literature, some of them from the Assyrian, Babylonian, and Egyptian hymns, and some of them from the Rigveda and the Zend-Avesta. They may also be paralleled, at least in the ascription of power and omniscience to the divine being, in many things told of the ruder races of mankind. These stand out from the common beliefs and practices of the ruder and even from the more civilized races of men, and we are puzzled to find an explanation of them. Be the explanation what it may, it was certainly a strenuous task to find an adequate conception of the power on whom men depended. That many mistakes would be made was to be expected, that the goal would be hard to reach is what might have been expected. That there should be many revolutions of thought and feeling, and many revolts, and many persecutions to put down revolt, may almost be taken for granted. For religion is the most precious possession of man, and in the history of it and its changes we find enlisted the deepest feelings, the strongest passions, the brightest and the darkest aspects of human nature, its fiercest bigotry and its deepest love. It is an intensified history of the ordinary story of human life, and the usual motives which actuate men are here disclosed with every tone accentuated. The object sought for is the highest, and the search is the most strenuous, of all human efforts.

The story of science is, also, one of errors and mistakes. In fact, it is not so long ago since science was in its infancy. The crudest notions of man, and of the world in which he lived, abounded, and one of

Rome's foremost poets, who felt that he was quite equal to the making of a world, and who was fierce in his criticism of the gods, believed that the sun was only a few feet in diameter. We may read what passed for science in many of the sciences; we may read of the Ptolemaic theory of the universe, of phlogiston, and of many other curiosities of the history of science, and yet we do not go to our scientific friends and urge these mistakes as reasons why the possibility of scientific truth should be doubted. In truth, science has to rewrite itself almost every generation. The conceptions of chemistry have been revolutionized within my own time. But the mistakes which science has made, and the imperfections which still cling to science, do not interfere with our belief in the existence of the objects with which science deals. Why should the mistakes which religion has made invalidate our persuasion of the great being who is the main object of religion? It is quite true that she has given forth in the course of time many partial, inadequate, even unworthy representations of the divine, but has not science given forth many inadequate and unworthy representations of nature? Has not nature been regarded as lawless, uncertain, capricious, and we have overcome that view, and look on nature now as an ordered system, moving under law. But have we not corrected the first attempts of men to set forth the idea of God, and have we not now come to some conception of the idea of God not altogether unworthy of Him who is the maker of heaven and earth? It does not seem to be a profitable exercise for science or religion to remember the sins and faults of youth, each of the other. Let each be judged by the achievements of their maturity, and by the promise of further progress of which they may hold out a reasonable hope.

Is it not time that the conflict should cease, or, at least, take another form? Is it not time to seek after something of a synthetic view, which shall gather together the elements contributed to the unified knowledge of the world in which we live and the power manifested in it, by all the sciences and philosophies and theologies, which represent the ripest achievement of human thought? Conflict and controversy may be the way, or one way, by which we attain to clearness of thought and lucidity of conception. Truth may advance in circles or curves, and advance may seem to be only retrogression, while it really moves in an upward spiral, toward a more complete form. Or there may have been an element neglected, necessary for the expression of the unity of truth, and that element may have to struggle for recognition, and its advocates may press it to the dislocation of the symmetry of the whole, and peace cannot be obtained till it finds due recognition. Looking back over the history of the struggle between competing ideals of life, between rival systems of philosophy, and opposing views of ethics, and contrasted systems of theology, we may find that each system has some elements worthy to have a place in the hierarchy of truth, fitted to represent the reality of things and persons in its adequate form. If our thoughts take a wider view and we look at the conflict between the scientific and the philosophic mind, and between both and the theological, we may ask ourselves whether these have not been looking at opposite sides of the shield? A mere syncretic method is not advocated by me. I do not wish to shovel together all the contradictory notions that have found a place in ethical, philosophical, and theological systems, and serve them up as the conciliation of differences, and the final product of rational investigation. Eclecticism and syncretism do not play an important part in the history of human thought. But cross-fertilization is an important process in biology, and has beneficial consequence.

May there not be cross-fertilization among the various organisms, the sum of which make up the organism of human knowledge, won by the protracted labour of the ages? May we not take from the physical sciences what they can tell us of the laws and methods of the working of the physical world? May we not familiarize our minds with the stupendous spectacle of the physical forces keeping step with one another, each in the service of the other, and all working in long-drawn harmony as elements in one system? Surely the service of these sciences ought to be recognized, and the greatness of the order made plain to us by them, the coördinated harmony of all the parts, and the order of the whole should give us some thought of the power manifested in and through them all. That gives one element in our thought of God. Our thought of Him must widen itself to the recognition of the stupendous power at work in the universe, working by methods which so far man has understood, though much is still beyond his conception. Science shows us a related world bound in a system, the changes of which take place in an orderly way, the rhythm of which may be understood. This vision of the order, beauty, and harmony of the world is the contribution of science to religion and theology. It matters not that once religion was suspicious of law and the reign of law, that it fondly lingered on the thought of a personal government of the world, which seemed also a capricious government. Religion has outgrown that mood, and it does not look for God in the absence of law, method, and order, it finds God in law, and rejoices in every discovery of science, and looks at such as a new discovery of the presence and the working of God. It still believes in a personal government of the world, but it has learned that will is steadfast and intelligent, not wilful and capricious.

Science has helped theology to purify and extend its thought of God. It was bound to do so, for it has revealed to us somewhat of the magnificence of the world in which we live. Lengthened in time and widened in space, filled with order and harmony in its onward sweep through the ages, the thought of all that science has disclosed must have widened our thought of God. Worlds beyond worlds and systems within systems, well our thoughts of the maker of the universe ought to be greater than the thoughts of those who believed this little planet was the centre of all the universe. But the main achievement of science is the discovery of law, at least this is its main achievement from the theological point of view. But science reveals to us still more as we wait and watch its work in the higher regions of its great endeavour. Through the ages one increasing purpose runs. Life prepared for, life appearing, life growing, developing, creatures appearing who are made to make themselves, and rational creaturehood appearing who develops the power of reading the story of the making of the world, all revealing a patient foreseeing intelligence content to labour and to wait in order to make a world fit to know, understand, and serve its maker. Biology makes its own contribution to the widening and deepening of our thought of God. He seems to win a way which can be understood, and, having once begun to work, He seems to keep to the method with which He began. It would seem as if the intelligent understanding of His work and His method was an object to Him. He worked in such a fashion as would disclose itself to the patient inquiry of finite intelligence. So the slow process of the evolution of life is a process of revelation, or a disclosure of the divine method of work, and thus a revelation of God.

It is, however, in relation to the character and the history of rational being that we come to a deeper revelation of God; or, to use another word which has not so technical a meaning, it is in connection with history that we have a deeper manifestation of God. Here we have larger discords yet a deeper harmony, more failures yet a higher success, mistakes innumerable in all departments of human action, yet each generation taking up the burden of the effort after truth, knowledge, and life, and working on in the hope of finding the kingdom of God. We need not again refer to the mistakes, failures, and sins of men through the generations, for, after all, too much may be said of them. Ethics slowly advanced, morality came to some consciousness of itself, philosophy came with its searching questions and its partial answers, criticism arose to try all that could be tried, and through the conflict and the struggle, the still, small voice of conscience made itself increasingly heard until the ripened thought of men came to have some idea of what a worthy conception of God ought to be. It was stern work which had to be done — not merely to advance from age to age, but to deal

with the attainments of former generations, to criticise inadequate conceptions which had not seemed
inadequate to a former generation, to rise above the
reluctance and unwillingness to disturb inherited beliefs, and to move onwards to the recognition of a
moral ruler, judge, and loving friend of men. It
was stern, and hard work, and it would not have
attained the success it did attain if there had been
no voice from beyond the veil and no pressure of
God in history.

The effort of philosophy is not merely man's
work; it is the work of God too. Theology owes
a large debt to philosophy; it has always used the
work of philosophy, and sometimes without due
acknowledgment.   But while religion and theology
owe a large debt to science and philosophy, and
have learned from them to deepen and widen their
thought of God and man, they still have their own work
to do, their own problem to solve, their own burden
to bear, and these are harder than any other problem.
They have to deal with the ultimate harmony and
unity of the universe, with the unity of all things in
the kingdom of God.   They do not look on the unity
and harmony as accomplished; rather, it is the
goal to be reached in the far future, when the
world is made which as yet is only in the making.
Religion and theology are grateful for the service
of science and philosophy, which have been of unspeakable service; they are grateful, too, for the in-

s

cessant criticism of these worthy friends — a criticism not always friendly, sometimes indeed very candid, bitter, and contemptuous, but they are thankful, notwithstanding. For it is of the utmost importance, in so high an endeavour, to have every belief tested to the uttermost, every assumption sifted, every argument criticised, that nothing weak or unworthy may be suffered to remain. For anything weak, unworthy, or unreasonable may have issues perilous to the success of the highest emprise ever undertaken by man. So we ask the help of science and philosophy for this great end, and we give the warning that we shall use their help for our own purpose. We do not seek a scientific or a philosophic solution of the problem, we have a deeper purpose than that. We will not accept from science merely an infinite and eternal energy, though we shall receive that as an element in our solution, nor will we accept from philosophy merely a universal substance, or a universal self-consciousness and nothing more, or any other of those substitutes for God which philosophy is fond of presenting to us, though we take their contributions as elements in our construction. We shall not rest until we find a God who will satisfy our religious needs, as well as our scientific and rational aspirations. It is not enough for us to arrive at infinite power, wisdom, even infinite goodness, we seek a God who can speak to us and to whom we can speak, a God who is something for Himself, as well as something for us, who can be the home of our life, and meet every aspiration, desire, and longing of the whole man.   It is because we believe that the being whom we call God is all that we have described, and more than we can describe, that we welcome all the help of science and philosophy; for we need all the help we can get to make any approximation to the work which man most sorely needs.

IX

PHILOSOPHY IN ITS AGNOSTIC ASPECT: ITS POSTULATES, ITS CHARACTER, AND ITS TRUTH

THE philosophies in vogue and influence at present are mainly of two types, and, while these types have many subsidiary forms, they are mainly two. In both the idea of evolution has a predominating influence, and plays a great part as an instrument for the solution of difficulties and as a fruitful point of view. True, they look at evolution from different ends of the telescope. The one philosophy of which the synthetic philosophy of Mr. Herbert Spencer may be taken as the type, looks at evolution from its simple and abstract beginnings, and seeks to deduce the actual world from them, by the use of such principles as "the instability of the homogeneous," "the multiplication of effects," and so on, and to some observers they seem to be engaged in the task of making something out of nothing. Evolution becomes the universal solvent, and in the last resort we must make any particular transition which is needed, under the threat that to suppose otherwise is to suppose that force does not persist. The other type of philosophy may be briefly described as idealism, of which there are many expositions, and many expositors in your country and in ours. It looks at evolution from the other end, and judges it from the point of view of the goal to which evolution tends. In fact, idealism rules in the most of our universities in England and in Scotland, and the philosophical voices of America set forth the idealist view with great eloquence and power and with persuasive force. The writers do not echo a British note, nor do they speak with a German accent; they have really done the work over again and have added to the idealist solution of the problem something distinctive and valuable. The typical name with us is that of Edward Caird, which is the most influential name in philosophy in Great Britain, and has been so for years.

What help toward a solution of the permanent religious question do we obtain from these dominant types of philosophy. Not much from Mr. Spencer. He leaves us in an attitude of reverence before an unknowable, and presents religion as a mystery which must always remain a mystery and nothing more. Once in a late part of the lengthened exposition of his system he seems to strike a more positive note, and gives an account of the object of religious veneration which is not merely negative. We have tried to read the " First Principles " in the light of the more recent exposition, and the last seems to go much farther than the first statement by him of the function and object of religion. They may be the same to Mr. Spencer, to me they seem to differ to the extent that the first statement is wholly negative, while the last is partly positive. We take the more positive statement. "That internal energy which, in the experience of the primitive man was always the immediate antecedent of changes wrought by him — that energy which, when interpreting external changes, he thought of along with those attributes of a human personality connected with it in himself; is the same energy which, freed from anthropomorphic accompaniments, is now figured as the cause of all external phenomena. The last stage reached is recognition of the truth that force as it exists beyond consciousness, cannot be like what we know as force within consciousness; and that yet, as either is capable of generating the other, they must be different modes of the same. Consequently, the final outcome of that speculation commenced by the primitive man is that the Power manifested throughout the Universe, distinguished and material, is the same Power which in ourselves wells up under the form of consciousness." (" Ecclesiastical Institutions," p. 839.) Another passage we quote, as it seems to leave us the hope that as evolution advances and man advances with it a knowledge of God may be within the reach of the developed man of the future. "Occupied with one or other division of Nature, the man of science usually does not know enough of the other divisions even rudely to conceive the extent and complexity of their phenomena; and supposing him to have adequate knowledge of each, yet he is unable to think of them as a whole. Wider and stronger intellect may hereafter help him to form a vague consciousness of them in their totality. We may say that just as an undeveloped musical faculty, able only to appreciate a simple melody, cannot grasp the variously entangled passages and harmonies of a symphony, which in the mind of composers and conductor are unified into involved musical effects awakening far greater feeling than is possible to the musically uncultured; so, by further more evolved intelligences, the course of things now apprehensible only in part may be apprehensible altogether, with an accompanying feeling as much beyond that of the present cultured man as his feeling is beyond that of the savage.

" And this feeling is not likely to be decreased but to be increased by that analysis of knowledge which, while forcing him to agnosticism, yet continually prompts him to imagine some solution of the great enigma which he knows cannot be solved. Especially must this be so when he remembers that the very notions, origin, cause, and purpose, are relative notions belonging to human thought, which are probably irrelevant to the Ultimate Reality transcending human thought; and when, though suspecting that explanation is a word without meaning when applied to this ultimate reality, he yet feels compelled to think there must be an explanation.

"But one truth must grow ever clearer, — the truth that there is an Inscrutable Existence everywhere manifested, to which he can neither find nor conceive either beginning or end. Amid the mysteries which become the more mysterious the more they are thought about, there will remain the one absolute certainty, that he is ever in presence of an Infinite and Eternal Energy, from which all things proceed." (pp. 842, 843.)

We are glad to receive from Mr. Spencer the assurance of one "absolute certainty," that there is an infinite and eternal energy, and that it stands in relation to all things, namely, that all things proceed from it. There is also something to be thankful for in the recognition of the fact that the power that manifests itself, distinguished as material, is the same power which in ourselves wells up under the form of consciousness. It would appear that agnosticism, even in the presence of the ultimate reality, is not absolute. It can, at least it does, make some assertions about the reality. It exists, it is infinite and eternal, it is manifested in the material world, it is manifested in consciousness, and the agnostic knows these two to be the same; and the agnostic can say that from this infinite and eternal energy all things proceed. The creed of agnosticism as set forth by Mr. Spencer is considerable. Far be it from us to seek to attenuate it, while we may wonder how on its own principles it came to make such assertions, — how do they reach the infinite and eternal, and how do they affirm the relationship between the ultimate reality and the finite manifestation of it? If the power is manifested, as Mr. Spencer says it is, is it not knowable, at least as far as it is manifested? If it is manifested in the material world and also in consciousness, can we not put these manifestations together, and say something true and adequate about the ultimate reality in addition to the propositions of Mr. Spencer? What is manifested is revealed, and the character of the thing is given by the manifestation, and we may speak about that.

In these passages quoted from Mr. Spencer, and in certain *obiter dicta* of his elsewhere, he opens out for us paths into the unknowable which we may safely tread, and following his example we may make for ourselves wider and longer paths than he would allow. In fact, that has been done for us by a distinguished follower of Mr. Spencer on this side. I do not know whether Mr. Fiske will allow me to call him a follower of Spencer, and so I will call him a distinguished exponent of a philosophy in many respects identical with the Spencerian philosophy. He has brought within limits the whole system of Spencer, and expressed it in clear and perspicuous language, and has brought within the reach of all, the leading principles of that philosophy which has many exponents at present, the greatest of whom is Mr. Fiske. His "Outlines of Cosmic Philosophy" has been familiar to me for years, and I read it yet. In the later part of the exposition Mr. Fiske seems to have worked at the subject of evolution for himself, and to have come to conclusions rather more positive than those of Mr. Spencer. In the Preface to his little book on the "Idea of God," Mr. Fiske says, "Nothing of fundamental importance in 'Cosmic Philosophy' needed changing, but a new chapter needed to be written, in order to show how the doctrine of evolution, by exhibiting the development of the highest spiritual human qualities as the goal toward which God's creative work has from the outset been tending, replaces man in his old position of headship in the universe, even as in the days of Dante and Aquinas. (The "Idea of God," Preface, p. 20.) To me as to other readers of "Cosmic Philosophy" it seemed that Mr. Fiske had left little room for theology except in the Spencerian sense, and he had certainly disposed of purpose in every sense of the term. His "Cosmic Philosophy" added nothing to the system of Spencer, and left us in the presence of an omnipresent energy. Like other readers, I welcomed that teleological passage, I am about to quote, and I do not care to inquire how much of "Cosmic Philosophy" would require to be rewritten to make it consistent with this and other passages. " The teleological instinct in man cannot be suppressed or ignored. The human soul shrinks from the thought that it is without kith or kin in all this wide universe. Our reason demands that there shall be a reasonableness in the constitution of things. This demand is a fact in our psychical nature as positive and irrepressible as our acceptance of geometrical axioms and our rejection of whatever controverts such axioms. No ingenuity of argument can bring us to believe that the infinite Sustainer of the universe will " put us to permanent intellectual confusion." There is in every earnest thinker a craving after a final cause; and this craving can no more be extinguished than our belief in objective reality. Our belief in what we call the evidence of our senses is less strong than our faith that in the orderly sequence of events there is a meaning which our minds could fathom were they only vast enough." (pp. 137-8.)

It would appear, therefore, that according to Mr. Spencer and to Mr. Fiske, there is a meaning in the universe, were our minds only great enough to grasp it. Mr. Spencer holds out a hope that in the future, whether distant or near he does not say, but in the future there may appear a mind to which the secret of the universe may be open, and Mr. Fiske has restored to us the hope of learning the meaning of the universe which is there already. Agnosticism is thus so far departed from by two of its greatest advocates. The unknowable has shrunk to smaller dimensions, and it is only the fear of anthropomorphism that seems to keep them from attenuating it still further. If a wider and stronger intellect may yet arise which may have a vague consciousness of the world in its totality, we may work on with the assurance that there is nothing in the totality considered in itself which makes it unknowable. Even human intelligence as it is, may come to have an apprehension of the meaning of the universe and its cause.

With anthropomorphism I have dealt elsewhere, and have endeavoured to show that all science and philosophy are anthropomorphic, and it is not possible for the human being to be other than anthropomorphic. Those who think they get beyond anthropomorphism have simply interpreted the universe in terms borrowed from the lowest parts of human experience. (See "Is God Knowable?" Chap. III.) It is largely from men who approach the problem from the scientific side that we hear the charge of anthropomorphism. For example, Mr. Graham in his "Creed of Science" puts the matter thus: "In particular this conception of God will not suit the theology that insists on ascribing to Him the attributes, at once metaphysical and specially human, of personality and consciousness; the former being the precise one that it is so difficult to get any clear conception of even in ourselves, and both, especially consciousness, being as Fichte and other philosophers have irrefutably demonstrated, inapplicable and directly contradictory to the notion of an Absolute Being. For consciousness and personality, whatever else they imply, clearly imply the notion of limits and conditions, neither of which can without contradiction be applied to an absolute and unconditioned Being, to a transcendent tremendous and universal power, the chief fact in our knowledge of which is precisely its freedom from the limits which govern and bind our finite being." (" Creed of Science," p. 364.) I have for a long time regarded with wonder and admiration sentences like the one now quoted, and many such may be culled from the pages of the current philosophies of this type. I have wondered that the writers of such sentences have not seen that they contradict themselves. At all events that they have fallen into confusion of thought, when they speak of being at all. Being is a determinate phrase, with a definite meaning, and that is a limitation. When they define it as power, that, on their own terms, is also a limitation. Still greater are the limitations set forth by the terms absolute, unconditioned, tremendous, and universal; from their point of view all these predicates involve limitations just as much as or more than is implied by consciousness and personality.

They proceed on the assumption that predicates are limitations, as in one sense they are, but from any rational point of view, to be is more than not to be, and the larger the number of predicates ascribed to a subject the greater is that subject. Deferring for a time the discussion of whether infinitude and personality are inconsistent with each other, let us ask what help we get from science that has become a metaphysic, toward an intelligent solution of the theistic question. From Mr. Spencer and Mr. Fiske there is some help, as we have pointed out already, in the insistence by them of the existence of a power to whose might we can set no limit. The whole of things proceeds from that infinitive and eternal energy. We are afraid that Mr. Spencer would go no further, and while he denies that we can infer anything of the power and the character of it from the manifestations within and beyond consciousness, he yet seems disposed to affirm that the power is immanent in the manifestations, and that the force is persistent along the lines of its manifestations, and has no other mode of persistence. It is, indeed, difficult to be sure of his meaning, and one can hardly say whether he has thought out the question. He is for the most part contented with the general assertion that the eternal power is unknowable. But Mr. Fiske has spoken on this very point and spoken to the purpose. "Hence to the query suggested at the beginning of this chapter whether the Deity can be identified with the Cosmos, we must return a very different answer from that returned by the Pantheist. The 'open secret,' in so far as secret, is God — in so far as open, is the world; but in thus regarding the ever changing universe of phenomena as the multiform revelation of an Omnipresent Power, we can in no wise identify the power with its manifestations. To do so would reduce the entire argument to nonsense. From first to last it has been implied that while the universe is the manifestation of Deity, yet is Deity something more than the universe. The doctrine which we have here expounded is, therefore, neither more nor less than theism, in its most pronounced, consistent, and unqualified form. It is quite true that the word 'theism,' as ordinarily employed, connotes the ascription of an anthropomorphic personality to the Deity." ("Cosmic Philosophy," Vol. II., p. 424.) Mr. Fiske, like Professor Graham, and all others who approach the question from the merely scientific side, will not allow us to ascribe the attributes of personality and consciousness to the deity. He is quite decided on that head. Again and again he tells us that "personality and infinity are terms expressive of ideas which are mutually incompatible. The pseud-idea, 'infinite person,' is neither more nor less than the pseud-idea circular triangle." (pp. 408–9.)

Thus, on the whole, while we gain something from the statement of Mr. Fiske that the deity is something more than the universe, we know nothing of what the "more" may be. We do not know, indeed, we may never know, whether we can ever come into the fellowship of the divine, or whether the divine can care for us; and the divine becomes for us on these terms a term from the meaning of which all thoughts of providence, guidance, government of the world, are rigidly excluded, as well as other notions more characteristic of religion. We are not prepared to pay so great a price, even for the doctrine of evolution, though we are persuaded that the doctrine of evolution is not essentially tied to the doctrine of the unknowable. That it is so is only the private opinion of Mr. Spencer and Mr. Fiske, and the evolutionary theory in its essentials may go along with the idea of a God who may be known and has made Himself known. The doctrine of the "unknowable" is the fruit of a theory of knowledge, and after that theory is removed, the gain we have got may still be retained. As we remarked already, the theory of Mr. Spencer and Mr. Fiske is refuted by their own practice. They define the "unknowable," and the one calls it an infinite and eternal energy, and the other calls it a power to which no limit in time and space is conceivable. In the use of these phrases they have transgressed against their own canons, and have ventured to speak of infinite and eternal in positive terms as if they had a real content which could be known as positive. What, then, becomes of the contention that the infinite and eternal are wholly negative? Are we to suppose that when we apply the words "infinite" and "eternal" to energy they negative the positive content of energy? Nay, for they merely negative the idea of any limit to the energy and the power. We have simply to carry out this statement of theirs in all directions and we get rid of a great part, of in fact the greatest part, of the agnostic argument. What right have they, on their own terms, to speak of the infinite and eternal in any way? They have no right to use negative terms to enhance a positive content.

Further, have they not transcended the limits of human knowledge, when they speak after this fashion, that is, the limits set by themselves? If they transcend the limit and extend our finite idea of force to its ideal, why find fault with me when I use the same privilege? If they raise power to its ideal and make it infinite, I am going to do the same thing, and to say there is an ideal of righteousness in the universe, there is truth eternal and beauty infinite and harmony unspeakable; and in fact I am just to take all I know of finite qualities, properties, and relations, and I am to raise them to their ideals, and hold them to be realized in the infinite and eternal being from which all things proceed. Why should these distinguished men be allowed to raise one property to its ideal because it suits their theory? and why should all others be characterized as anthropomorphic if they use the same privilege? But I do not press the *argumentum ad hominem*, there is something better to do.

Let us look back from the point where Mr. Spencer leaves us, and let us also look round and up to find what worlds he has taken away. Taking the great scientific movement of thought which may be represented by Mr. Spencer, let us observe how far it has brought us and where it leaves us. We had thought that we had stood in the middle world of being, with God above us and the world beneath us, and in most intimate relations with both, and we thought that the full interpretation of our own experience would give us the key to the knowledge of what is beneath us, of what is around us, and of what is above us. Well, but with the advance of science, and specially with the coming of the theory of evolution, we are left in the sad predicament that, while there may be something above us, we can never know what it is. Our highest and our best are expressly shut out from the exercise of any function in the ultimate interpretation of the universe. Our kinship with what is beneath us is fully brought out, and great stress is laid on it, no doubt to our advantage, for all truth is beneficial. A vast body of truth has been brought home to us; we are sharers in countless structures, organs, and functions with the grades of being beneath us. The world of nature cannot be regarded as alien to us, and whether we were moulded out of the dust or evolved by slow degrees through an ascending series of lower beings, in either case we must feel a true kinship with all that is beneath us, and a true reverence for it. Our knowledge of all that is beneath us has come in like a flood, wave upon wave, in all the sciences, and as a consequence our thoughts in general and of the methods by which truth may be known are dominated by the methods and the aims which have been so successful in this single region of truth. Thus we are inclined to judge of ourselves and of all that is above us by methods and measures taken from things below us. This tendency grows by what it feeds on, and the explanation of the universe by what is below man strives to become complete, coherent, and exhaustive.

The most complete expression of this tendency is to be found in the works of Mr. Spencer and Mr. Fiske. While they formally protest that there may be something higher than intelligence at work in the world, as a matter of fact every principle of explanation found in their works has been drawn from the world beneath man. The persistence of force is the foundation principle, and from it all is derived. As we advance in the process of explanation there are introduced successive simplicities, which form the elements which by differentiation and integration proceed on their way to further complications; and so the story goes on until we come to the perfectly

evolved society of Mr. Spencer as set forth in the
"Data of Ethics." Here is an evolution up to man,
and no further. Measures and procedures taken exclusively from the world below us are held sufficient
for the explanation of things, and even the fruit and
flower of personal and social life are derivatives from
what is below us. Man is left with no higher, with
nothing nobler than himself. But is there not the
infinite and eternal energy left to us, and the blind
and blank adoration of the unknowable? Yes, but is
that higher, greater, nobler than I am? No, for an
infinite that does not know itself, that has no purpose,
no aim, no way of making itself known, is not higher
than man, it is lower. The theory of Mr. Spencer
is not even zoömorphic, it is drawn solely from
physics. Or rather it is drawn from the lowest
aspect of human experience, that of our simplest
experience of resistance.

Still there is the irresistible belief that we do stand
in the middle between what is below and what is above
us, and the knowledge of this belief must lead us
upwards or downwards. Man always has found it
difficult to be upright when he has disregarded the
knowledge of God. Take away that ideal and man
immediately becomes retrogressive. It was always so,
and it is more so to-day. Formerly he thought he
was a being apart, separate from the other beings of
the earth, separately formed, able to pursue a separate destiny. But now he finds that in his physical

structure he is not widely separate from what is lower, and in many other respects he is closely akin to the higher animals, and the full force of these scientific discoveries press upon him to his undoing, if he cannot reënforce his conviction of his uniqueness by considerations of endowments shared by none of the other creatures. To restore him to himself, to lift him upwards, and to enable him to realize that better and higher self after which he aspires, there is needed the sure hope of the knowledge of an actual God in whom is realized the ideal of truth, life, knowledge, and action, who alone can raise him to the goal which he dimly foresees as possible, and which he longs to make real.

Thus we need to supplement the story of the evolution up to man, by the story of a moral evolution of man up to the ideal he has attained, and to show that the story of ethical evolution has a method and law of its own. There is also the story of spiritual evolution to be told, whereby man has so far reached the stage of self-knowledge, self-reverence, and self-control. There is still more the story of religious evolution, a more difficult story to tell though inextricably interwoven with the others, — the story of the purification and elevation of man's belief in God until he came to believe in the living God, the maker of heaven and earth, the upholder of all that is, the source, the guide, and the goal of all things, of whom, for whom, and through whom are all things. Nor do

I believe that the process of evolution in any sphere has taken place without the help of Him Whom they call the unknowable Power from which all things proceed. The activity of the Eternal, call Him by what name you may, is the postulate of every theory of evolution. It is so when you have attenuated it to the idea of persistence. And it is much more so when you give to the conception of God its full value. Why, I ask, forbid us to find the realization of all our ideals in the infinite and the eternal, when you have permitted yourselves to realize your ideal of energy in the infinite and the eternal? I do not find any worthy answer to that question, and no answer at all save a reference to a theory of knowledge which makes knowledge impossible.

In the experience of mankind, so far back as we have any knowledge of that experience, there is the belief in a higher power, on whom man felt his dependence, and that power was believed to be a power making for righteousness, interested in truth, working for the growth of goodness, taking measures for the suppression of wrong-doing, and evil of all kinds. There is a belief in a righteous ruler of the world who had the right and the authority to govern, and the right, also, to enforce his will by the most terrible sanctions. The actual government of the world of men, as it can be traced through history, seemed to confirm that belief, and to show an actual government of the world according to ethical law.

The power above us was on the side of virtue, goodness, truth, and righteousness; and on the reading of events, through a lengthened period, it seemed to hold true that where the ethical qualities of self-restraint, self-government, by high aims and purposes, purity, goodness, love, and other ethical qualities have become less and less, there followed consequences of a grave and miserable kind. The presages of conscience seemed to be confirmed by the actual facts of human experience as these are recorded in history.

Then there are the reflections of man on his own life in its intellectual, ethical, and religious aspects as these were present in his experience. It seemed to him that intellectually he was related to an external world, in intercourse with which his life of feeling, thinking, and activity came to fruition. The existence of an external world, in connection with which he could realize his purpose and his character, became one of his assured beliefs, and in acting on that belief his life became one of realized activity. However we may interpret the external world, it is confessedly there, and in intercourse with it life realizes itself. But the external world does not exhaust the beings with whom we have intercourse. There is the world of our fellow-men, who are more to us, and who play a larger part in the evolution of our personality, than is accomplished by our fellowship with the external world. From man we obtained language to enable us to think and to give expression to our thought, lessons of experience not transmitted by mere hereditary descent, but handed down as a treasure of human feeling, aspiration, achievement, a record of noble aims and deeds expressed in thoughts that breathe and words that burn; we obtained in addition the love that blessed our infancy, the care that guarded our youth, the patient forethought that planned and carried out our education, the wise affection that looked forward to our future and taught us the habit of obedience to what was wiser and better than we, as the sure way to self-control and to a life of fruitful endeavour and assured work, the atmosphere charged with the tradition of the ages, which we breathed in our home, in the school, college, university; these and many other influences played on us and helped to make us what we are, and are we to question or doubt the reality of those intellectual, ethical, and spiritual influences? No, we do not doubt the existence and validity of these.

But pass on now and inquire into the validity of the object on which our religious life is fed, and you meet with a different mode of treatment of that object. Nay, it is not our religious life alone, it is our higher ethical life as well that has its postulates called into question. One of the postulates of our moral life is that we are in relation to an objective moral authority of perfect holiness, goodness, righteousness, and love, who has the right to control us, guide us, cherish us, and reward us. Without this postulate the infinite character of duty is never adequately realized. Without this objective authority who has the right to command our conscience, we can never rise to the great height of our moral calling, and the word "ought" without this authority will never reach its transcendent significance. We may try — it has been often tried — to attenuate the meaning of the word "ought," to substitute for its categorical imperative some lesser derivative, such as, if you desire the end you must use the means; or it may be contended that the oughtness that constrains a man is the inherited custom of countless generations; but after it is attenuated so it comes back in its august authoritativeness, and confronts us with its awful benignity and says, "You ought." And we bow in silence before the majesty of moral law, and recognize in our best moments that this is the voice of the supreme. Duty is itself infinite. I appeal to the voice of our consciousness, and I ask how is it that we feel that we can never realize our ideal of duty, how is it that we find that ideal growing as we climb higher, that the more we attain the farther removed from us seems the ideal of duty which is our ideal? This is the universal testimony of the human consciousness, that, no matter what the ideal of life and duty is, or may be, whether it be that of the cultured or the uncultured, he finds himself ever baffled in his striving to attain it.

Is not this one of the pathways that lead to God,

and one of the infinites which God has put within
the human heart? What is this ideal of duty, this
imperative feeling of obligation, this conscious con-
straint that bids us to go on even when we have
found our most earnest strivings baffled, and our
best efforts ineffective, unless it is the call to us of
an infinite perfection that really cares for us, and
the prompting of a love that is supreme, that we
should remember our eternity, and be worthy of
bearing the responsibility of being a rational, self-
conscious, ethical, and spiritual being, who can by
divine help determine himself to the realization of his
ideal in character and life. It is a great position, this
of a rational self-conscious, ethical being, and the
risk of failure in the trial to realize the personality is
great. It is the task of all of us. To live is, indeed,
for all of us, to form ideals and to fall short of them,
and ever to realize that there is a contrast between
what is and what ought to be. In all spheres of
human activity this is so, we can never state a truth
in all its fulness and accuracy, nor put into form the
beauty that haunts us; we labour to make our practical action embody our ideal of what a perfect action
ought to be, and we fail; we cannot even write as we
see we ought to do; and in our moral action and life
the good that we would we do not, and the imperfections and defects we would avoid, if we could,
cling to us through all our life.

Yet to our finite and baffled existence there comes

the persuasion that there is a complete and perfect life, a grander world than the present, a conviction that this world and this life is not the whole. Our ideals imperatively demand realization. Our imperfect knowledge leads us to the hope that there is a knowledge that is perfect, an explanation that makes the rationality of the whole apparent to a mind for which the whole is. The isolated fragments of our existence, even in their isolation, cause us to think of a complete and perfect beauty and symmetry, in which the visions of harmony and beauty that dimly float before the imaginations of the best and purest of the sons of men have their complete fulfilment. Beauty and harmony, grace of outline and harmony of parts, are with us here, and our æsthetic convictions demand a sphere in which they will be satisfied. Above all, in the moral sphere man sees a hand that beckons, a vision that invites, an ideal that draws him on, and on the reverse side a pure and holy power that warns and sternly forbids those actions and inclinations that lead men to become false to the highest moral ideal they know. Thus while we are in the midst of the perishing, the transient, and fragmentary, we are so constituted as to demand the imperishable, the abiding, and the whole; in one word, man's greatest need is God, in whom all ideals meet and are realized.

We need God on all sides of our manifold life, — intellectually, æsthetically, morally, religiously. God alone can draw forth all the powers of man into harmonious action. If one may use the phrase, God is the environment of man, in intercourse with whom man can attain to perfection. Shall the need of man for the infinite and the eternal be limited merely to one aspect, and that not the highest? Shall we say that there is energy, and declare all else to be unknowable? Are we to look up to a lonely universe, and in all the higher spheres of being be driven to think that we have no kith and kin in the world above us? Is the world above and beyond us, as Shelley says, "A wide, gray, lampless, dark, unpeopled world?" No, the history of humanity, sad though it be, proves that there is a Being who is above them, interested in them, caring for them, who allowed Himself to be thought of by them in such forms and terms as they could use to describe the highest and the best, and from that lowly and inadequate beginning strove to lead them onwards and upwards to higher, truer, and more adequate thoughts and conceptions of Him. In the earlier days men sought for their highest and best in the external world of nature, and seemed to exhaust the possibilities of earth and sea and sky, in order to find a fitting expression for the Divine; and they were not satisfied, for the world-idea could not adequately represent the Divine. Then they turned to the idea of their own intelligent, social, and ethical life, and sought for the highest and best conceptions wrought in them by their personal, social, and civic life, and strove to think of the Divine in terms borrowed from these ideals. It did not satisfy, though it led them to worthier thoughts of God. There was something gained when the phenomena of personal, social, and state life were taken as the material of their thought of God, for it led them to think of God as the meaning of the social union, its source, and its goal. The actual life of man in social union led to that thought which we find in Greek and Roman civilization, that gods and men formed one community, and were in relation to each other.

But the growing intelligence of men, and their higher organization, and their advancing morality, led them on to further striving. Religion is not satisfied with the solutions of intelligence, nor with the sanctions of ethics, nor with that conception of God which, perhaps, might satisfy our speculative, our æsthetic, and our ethical activity. She must find a God who realizes her own ideal. So in every age religion, while taking note of all that is accomplished in science, philosophy, and ethics, sets men to work anew, for she must solve the problem from her own point of view, with her own postulates, and from her own data. The work must be done over again, and she is not satisfied until she has worked up the material derived from the sciences and philosophies into a new and higher synthesis which is all her own. She is not contented with a philosophy of religion, nor will she consent to be reduced to an aspect of philosophy; rather her imperious and imperative demand is that science and philosophy shall toil in her service. For religion is highest and most central, and has, or ought to have, the controlling position in life. Religion is the sanction of morality; yes, but it is more than the sanction of morality. When it becomes a mere sanction of morality, it fares ill with religion and morality. Philosophy may be satisfied with such a conception of God as will help her to solve the problems of thought and life which are confessedly philosophical; science may be satisfied with such a conception of God as will help her to conceive the order of the universe, and help her to think of the realm of law as real; and ethics may be contented with the recognition of moral law as issuing forth from a sovereign, of infinite power and wisdom, who has imposed an ethical law on all intelligent agents as the condition of their existence in a realm of rational beings. But a God who is only the cause of order, the presupposition of knowledge, the source of moral order, is utterly insufficient to satisfy the religious demands of man.

So religion ever sets men to toil anew in order to reach God, if haply they can find Him. Men must find God, and the God we find must satisfy all our needs; the craving for guidance, the thirst for righteousness, the striving after truth, and the longing for purity. Specially does religion demand a God who is something, and can do something, who can come near to men in a personal way, and speak to them words which they can understand. Here we come to the crux of the whole matter, to that point where religion must ever take her stand, and absolutely refuse to accept the solutions pressed on her acceptance by science and philosophy. What some of these are we shall see in the concluding chapter. At present our aim is to say that religion can never accept a solution that casts the world into the life of God, and makes the states and changes of the world to be states and changes of Him. God is for religion more than the universe, and He has ways of activity and of manifestation not measured by the movements of the universe, and not limited by its ongoing. In other words, a postulate of religion is the transcendence of God.

No doubt the task is a tremendous one that religion sets to man. We recognize, also, that science and philosophy have not made the performance of the task an easy one. But it is a task to which we must gird ourselves generation after generation. We try to think it is possible to construct a thought of God, as One in Whom all things and persons live and move and have their being, and yet as a God who has a life in Himself, for Himself, and to Himself. It is comparatively easy to reach the immanence of God in the world; in fact, that conception has been reached by many routes, in many ways. That mysterious power which is both the path and the path goers, which is everything and nothing, meets us in the speculations of Laotze, in the existence without a predicate, which is an Indian form of mysticism; and on the subjective side, meets us again in the self of all selves, meets us in the *anima mundi*, and in a thousand other forms in the history of speculation, ancient and modern. It is not a solution hard to reach, for it has been reached so often, and reappears so frequently in the history of human thought. Religion is never satisfied with a pantheistic solution, let it take whatsoever form it may. For religion must have a God who can speak, who can reveal Himself, not only as the power by whom planets gravitate and stars shine, by whose strength the worlds are maintained in being, and living things have their life and activity, but religion demands a Being, who, though He is not an object among other objects, yet is still an object.

Thus religion must look at the problems and solutions of science and philosophy from its own point of view, and in the light of its own imperative needs. And she has as good a right as they; the only relevant question is can she make her contention good? At all events, religion has under the guidance of her own postulates entered into human life, transformed and transfigured it, and made it holy, sacred, and august. She has made every man feel, as nothing else has made him feel, that life is a sacred trust, given to him for eternal ends; that there is a purpose for every man which every individual must realize for himself and in himself, or otherwise it will never be realized. No one else can take the place of any man, no one can do his work, and if he be a failure, the wealth of the universe is so far lessened. This purpose is not formed by the man himself, he feels that it is formed for him by Another with whom he has to do, and it is gradually revealed to him as he faithfully strives to follow the light and do the work which he recognizes he must do. In his life calling, in his daily work, whatever that work may be, a man whom religion has grasped, feels that he is in the presence of One high, pure, holy, to Whom he belongs, Whose authority is absolute, Whose power is sovereign, and Whose care over him is most minute, and Whose interest in him is unspeakable. This is one of the most familiar of human experiences, and who shall say that it has no roots in reality?

Suppose, then, we take this as an actual experience, and ask ourselves how religion may state its demands? Let us think of one omnipotent, all-wise, all-loving, who in power, love, and wisdom made the worlds, and who set Himself to make a creation to which He could communicate Himself. This is the central thought of your great American thinker, Jonathan Edwards, who ever strove to set forth God as a Being who strives to communicate Himself to His creation. Looking back on the history of the creation as we are able to read it, it may be fruitfully looked at as the story of the making of a world, which could receive the self-communication of the living God. God gave Himself to the universe as the universe was able to receive Him. To the inorganic world as immanent power and order, to the organic world as life, growth, and purpose, to the world made in His own image, He gave Himself as intelligence, self-consciousness, self-guidance, ethical purpose and freedom, and above all as the religious spirit of truth and love and grace, so that when they attained to purity of heart they might see God.

Religion is thus not without a view and a purpose and a goal. For it looks back on the history of the past as a story of divine toil and striving toward the making of a world to which God could communicate Himself and which would have the capacity of receiving Him. This is a kind of world which could not be produced by a fiat, if, indeed, any world could be. It is a kind of world which could only be made by its own coöperation. To take it in its highest reaches, the world to which God could communicate Himself, is a world of ethical, self-conscious beings, who under the leading of a divine training and education, through discipline and trial, would build themselves to a character, and mould themselves on an ideal made known to them, and who would be persuaded that they were made for God and that they could be themselves only when they found themselves in God. Thus religion regards the unity of things not as accomplished or real in the past or in the present; it lies before her vision as a goal to be accomplished in the future when the making of the world is complete, and a creation is formed that can be filled with all the fulness of God. Religion must find a way of conceiving the relation of God to the world which will conserve the freedom of God and leave Him free to enter into these closer relations with a people fitted to receive them, which can represent that fellowship which alone deserves the name of religion.

We do not in any way interfere with the work of science, which is based on the intelligibility and rationality of the universe, nor do we say anything against the striving of philosophy to think the universe as one, and to regard it as a related system existing for thought. We simply take care of our own postulates, and say to them that religion cannot, will not, place the world-idea in the position of the idea of God. We must ever hold that these are distinct. As we saw, Mr. Spencer, finding that the belief in immortality and the belief in God have ever gone together in human history, has insisted that one of them should be derived from the other, so science and philosophy have insisted that the idea of the world and the idea of God should be identified, and this has in fact been the real issue of the age-long controversy which religion has had to wage for its existence. It is the issue to-day. Never in the history of human thought has the identification of the world-idea with the idea of God been presented in so alluring and persuasive a form as at the present hour. Never has philosophy taken so fair and fascinating a form as it does now, and never has it given so generous a recognition to the moral, social, and religious ideals of men. Never has philosophy insisted so strongly on the truth, beauty, and worth of the highest ideals of religion as under the inspiration of Hegel, one of the greatest, if not the greatest, of philosophic thinkers. But while we gladly admit and, indeed, assert this, and much more than this, we must sadly turn to our own path and take up the burden of our own work; for the idealistic philosophy makes religion to be simply an aspect of itself, and does not leave us a God into whose fellowship we may enter, in whose service we may find perfect freedom. For we can come to Him, and He can come to us, only by the way of the works He has made, by the institutions He has founded, and by the ways of the universe which is His only manifestation. We need a God who can speak to us, and if He cannot speak directly to us, the greater and better part, the flower and fruit of religion will wither and die.

X

IDEALIST PHILOSOPHY: ITS MERITS AND ITS DEFECTS; THE CONCEPTION OF GOD; HOW SHALL WE CONCEIVE THE SYNTHETIC UNITY OF GOD, MAN, AND THE WORLD?—THE KINGDOM OF GOD

RELIGION is possible only if man feels that he is related to God. A God above us, but also a God who is within us, is a perennial belief of man, common to all religions. It has obtained the most complete expression in the highest religion known, Christianity, yet it has been present in every religion. God as the universal father and all men as His children, this is the expression of the relationship between God and man. It is the general expression of the relationship that we take at present, without entering on the particular doctrines that articulate it into a scheme. Nor at this stage do we dwell on the proof of the statement that this appears in every religion. For this has received proof in almost every book dealing with the history of religions. We may take it for granted here.

The relationship between God and man, which is a postulate of the religious life, has found various forms of expression, and has demanded many means for its satisfaction. The need for fellowship is imperative. Yet as religious thought advanced, and the conception of God advanced with the growth of human intelligence and character, the difficulty of fellowship appeared to become greater and greater. For God seemed to become farther and farther removed from man in proportion as man conceived Him in higher and higher terms. He became in man's conception of Him, the all-knowing, almighty, all-present One, in Whom all things lived and moved and had their being, and His ethical attributes became more and more distinct ; justice, holiness, righteousness, truthfulness, and love came to be predicated of Him, and these conceptions of Him grew with the religious experience of men, until they found it difficult to conceive the possibility of communion with God. The higher the conception of God, the greater is the difficulty of conceiving the possibility of fellowship and communion. The heavens of heavens cannot contain Him, shall He indeed dwell with man on the earth ? This is an ancient expression of the difficulty, and yet a religious solution of it came to these old thinkers. He whom the heaven of heavens could not contain, became a dweller in the human heart. This solution was reached by an ancient people, who had somehow attained to the highest thought of God reached by the ancient world, who thought of the worlds as formed by the word of God, Who spake and it was done, Who commanded and it stood fast, who held fast both to the transcendence of God, and to His dwelling with men, and His indwelling in them. O God, thou art my God, though at the same time the worshipper knew that God was everywhere. Communion with God a necessity of the worshipper, though how it was possible to think out the possibility of such fellowship was not clear. In fact, these ancient people had the same difficulty which weighs on us to-day, namely, to think of fellowship between an eternal, infinite being, and man the creature of a day. But such a fellowship is necessary if religious life is not to die. A man must be persuaded that he is near to God, and that God is near to him. Men have had that persuasion, and the records of religious experience tell us that they have had a conviction of fellowship with God of so vivid and real a kind as to change their conduct and purify their life. The record of such experience is so wide and so common, that it is as well attested as any experience can be. There must have been a way whereby God could have come to man, for the records prove the reality of this communion.

Again, the religious life demands that the living God, with Whom man has fellowship, shall be no abstraction, Who has no power or movement in Himself, with no character and no attributes, but a real living power, Who can be an object to our devotion, our affection, Who can call forth our desires and reward them ; and be the theoretical difficulties of construing such an object what they may, man will continue to act on this belief. You say that God is not an object among other objects, but He is the subject for which all objects are. Well, religion, with imperturbable conviction, makes reply, and says, yes; God is the subject for which all objects are, but He is also an object for me with whom I have come into communion, and He has spoken to me. Religion makes the further request to science and philosophy, had you not better try to conceive a kind of unity which will enable me to look at all things in God, and God in all things, and yet maintain that God is something for Himself, and something directly for me? Have you exhausted the possible kinds of unity?

Still more imperative becomes the need of religion, when we come face to face, not merely with the facts of human weakness and finitude, but face to face with the awful fact of the consciousness of sin and guilt, the most inexplicable and the saddest of human experiences, if there is no fellowship with God. It does not help me much to be told that error is only one side of truth, and is done away with by being included in a wider truth, nor that sin is merely defect, because, in my consciousness of guilt, there is the persuasion that I have broken that personal bond which subsisted between the holy God and me, and I can have no abiding peace till the fellowship is restored. Guilt arises from the consciousness of kinship with God, and from the feeling that I have proven untrue to that kinship. This is also a universal human experience, and must, therefore, have its roots in reality.

I do not dwell further on the demands which religion makes on our thinking; these are named just to show that any philosophical construction of the unity of things must be widened in order to do justice to the religious experience of man. It was in this relation that the great system of Hegel came to grief, broke up into a right and a left and a centre party. Hegel did really try to do justice to the religious experience of man. He did believe that his system was theorized Christianity, and he spoke beautifully of the synthetic unity which religion brought to the life of the common man. His system did for the thinker what religion had already done for the man in the street. But alas! the experience of the common man refused to be theorized in the Hegelian way. The position set forth was that religion and philosophy were different in form, but in matter and aim they were one. Philosophy was religion in the form of thought, reasoned, articulated, set forth in such a way as to be wholly explicated, and understood. Religion is philosophy as the Vorstellung, and its truth is set forth in institutions, customs, rites, and it is always embodied in some symbolical way. The history of religions is the description of the way in which religion was able to embody in partial forms, more or less complete, the truth that it was able to grasp. Finally the absolute religion was reached, and Christianity was able to grasp on its own side and embody in its own way that absolute truth which on its side philosophy, in the hands of Hegel, had also accomplished.

Hegel set to work on these lines, and made a manful attempt to translate the facts and doctrines of Christianity into the language of the Hegelian system. The Christian doctrine of the Trinity became the whole of philosophy and the essence of religion. Thesis, antithesis, synthesis, the tripartite movement, which expressed the dialectic evolution of the universe, easily applied itself to the doctrine of Father, Son, and Spirit, and immediately there arose schemes which dealt with the kingdom of the Father, the kingdom of the Son, and the kingdom of the Spirit; for the Father is God as He exists in and for Himself, in eternity, and the Son is God as He exists as other, in time, and the Spirit is the other returning to oneness, bearing with it the reconciliation accomplished in the process. The Hegelian dialectic movement entailed immense labour on its advocates. It was necessary for them to apply the dialectic movement to nature, to history, to religion, and to show that the facts of nature, the world of life, the phenomena of human history, and the world of religion could be read in that way. The attempt to do so led to many luminous and instructive and suggestive views; but the facts were somewhat stubborn and refractory, and the Hegelian philosopher was sometimes not well acquainted with science, or history, or religion, and to the reader of their works the facts and events seemed to be on a bed of Procrustes. On all sides there was a revolt against this idealism. Men of science neglected the theory and turned to other work, philosophy also turned away, and religion, in particular, found that its most important interests were in danger. It was in this relation that the matter came to a crisis. Strauss applied the Hegelian method to the facts on which Christianity based her belief. No doubt Hegel had himself done so, but cautiously and generally; but Strauss, persuaded at that time of the truth and adequacy of the Hegelian philosophy, sought to translate the doctrine of Christianity into Hegelian formulæ. The outcome of the transformation is found in the " Leben Jesu " and in the " Domatik " of Strauss, which I shall not describe, as they are familiar to every student. But the publication of the " Leben Jesu " was the signal for the outburst of the storm, and the signal for the separation of the Hegelian school into the three parties of the right, the centre, and the left. A full account of the separation and its results for modern thought and life, will be found in Siebert's " Geschichte de neueren Deutschen Philosophie seit Hegel," an able and candid work. See also Fairbairn's " Christ in Modern Theology."

My limits will not permit me to enter on the his-

tory of the modern tendencies toward idealism. The
modern idealists in our country and in yours agree in
saying that the work has all to be done over again,
and with fuller knowledge of science in all its departments, and of the facts and events of history, and of
the meaning and worth of religion. To myself their
efforts have been very significant, and they have been
able to fertilize all modern inquiry, and to set every
problem in a new light. There is no sphere in which
their influence is not to be traced. They have helped
us to place evolution, which seems to be in the air, in
a light which enables us to accept it without accepting the evolution of something out of nothing. They
have enabled us to look with fresh interest on the
history of habits, customs, institutions, from the
rudest to the most complex, and they encourage us
to look forward to a goal not yet reached, a goal
which will conserve the gain won by the toil of all
the ages. Why, then, not accept idealism as the
crown and the hope of theology and philosophy. In
some respects I do accept it. I accept it in so far
as they tell me that mind is first in the universe, and
that the universe has a meaning. I accept it when
they tell me of experience and the rise within experience of the distinction of subject and object, and of
the truth that all objects are for the subject. I
follow gladly, as they take this living, breathing,
concrete self of mine, and show me that the analysis
of this real self and of the conditions of its life,

thought, and action, gives, or imperatively demands, the cosmos, that is to say, they show me that my experience is possible only if I am in a rational world, to which I am related, and which is related to me. The world they show me is not a huge contemporaneity, but an ordered world, each part related to each, and all bound together in relations which can be thought. I follow on as they lead me into the ethical world, and watch with admiration their theoretical construction of the possibility of moral experience, and obey as they tell me how the self is to be realized. Nor do I dissent, though I hesitate, as they proceed to show that as from the side of the finite self a cosmos is needed and is given as the presupposition of experience, so on the other side a cosmos demands a mind for which it is. But here I falter and tread with a hesitating step. For I look at the representations of the subject, for which all subjects are, and I do not find that the conceptions set forth by recent idealists meet the conditions of the case.

To begin with Mr. Bradley: "The absolute has no history of its own, though it contains histories without number. These, with their tale of progress or decline, are constructions starting from and based on some one given piece of finitude. They are but partial aspects in the region of temporal appearance. Their truth and reality may vary much in extent and in importance, but in the end it can never be more than relative." ("Appearance and Reality," p. 499.) Again, "The absolute is not personal, nor is it moral, nor is it beautiful or true." (p. 533.) In a rather condescending tone he says: "Religion prefers to put forth statements which it feels are untenable, and to correct them at once by counter-statements, which it finds are no better. It is then driven forwards and backwards between both, like a dog which seeks to follow two masters. A discrepancy worth our notice is the position of God in the universe. We may say that in religion God tends always to pass beyond Himself. He is necessarily led to end in the absolute, which for religion is not God." (p. 466.) The climax of this argument is found in a footnote to page 450. It leads to the dilemma: "If God is, I am not, and if I am, God is not. We have not reached a true view until the opposite of this becomes self-evident. Then, without hesitation, we answer that God is not Himself, unless I also am, and that, if God were not, I certainly should be nothing."

It is somewhat difficult to follow the reasoning of Mr. Bradley, and exceedingly difficult to know what God stands for in the sentence we have quoted. For him the reality is experience; so he calls it frequently. It has no history, though it contains histories without number. Changes are ever going on within that "experience," and yet that experience knows no changes. But the main difficulty I feel in dealing with the idealistic solution in all its forms is that the unity they reach is a quantitative one. It is so with Mr. Bradley, it is so with the Master of Balliol, with Professor Wallace, with Green, and with all who work under their influence. The experience of Mr. Bradley is the union of subject and object in the underlying unity set forth in the "Gifford Lectures" of Edward Caird, or it is the all-inclusive self-consciousness of Green which realizes itself in finite consciousness. The objection to all of these representations is just that they are quantitative, and that they cannot do justice to the reality of finite experience.

To do justice to the work of Edward Caird, we quote the following: "If, in accordance with the principles of Idealism, we regard the infinite not as an abstraction, but as a self-determining principle; if we follow out the doctrine of the correlation of inner and outer experience, and if we interpret that doctrine in the light of the idea of evolution and the consequences which have been drawn from it, viz. that nature comes to self-consciousness in man, and that, therefore, the process of man's life is a continuation of the self-revelation of the Absolute Being which begins in nature, — it then becomes possible to think of God as the principle of unity in all things, and yet as a living God in whose image man is made. And, on the same view, it becomes possible to think of Man as 'a partaker in the divine nature,' and, therefore, as a self-conscious and self-determining spirit, without gifting him with an absolute individuality, which would cut him off from all union and communion with his fellow-creatures and with God. I do not deny that there are many difficulties in this view, difficulties with which I have not attempted to deal. But it seems to me this is the only line of thought which makes it possible to escape the opposite absurdities of an *individualism* which dissolves the unity of the universe into atoms, and an abstract *monism* which leaves no room for any real individuality either in God or in man; not to speak of the still greater absurdity of holding *both* of these one-sided views at once." ("The Evolution of Religion," Vol. II., p. 84.)

The problem is to obtain such a conception of God, the cosmos, and man as will enable us to think them in their relations each to each, the relative reality of each, and how to construe the reality as a unity. What kind of unity is it to be? For some kind of unity must be reached, or we shall be driven to despair of knowledge and of life. An abstract unity is not sufficient, it dissolves in our hands on a moment's serious examination. Neither force, energy, nor substance can stand the strain of criticism, for it is impossible to get these to move, or to translate themselves into the concrete reality of experience. Nor does any other simplicity I have been able to meet in the history of philosophy help me to think of the unity in variety which makes up the universe. A universal self-consciousness, or the unity of subject and object, is no more an adequate conception than the persistence of force. Nor will the experience of Mr. Bradley meet the case. In truth, we must arrive at a conception which leaves room for real individuality, that will recognize the uniqueness of every person, and yet place every person in relation to every other person and thing, that is, has been, or will be. It must allow reality to history, and permit a real progress and real events in it. It must recognize human activity as a factor in the world's history, and recognize somehow that good and evil, happiness and misery, righteousness and sin, are not appearance, but stern realities which philosophy and theology must deal with. The cosmos is not appearance, man is real, and God is no abstraction.

The great question of theism to-day is not contained in a discussion of the various proofs elaborated by the diligence of former thinkers, nor in the criticism of these, which is so commonplace ever since the epoch-making work of Kant. The proofs and the criticism can be found in many volumes, and on both not much that is new or profitable can now be said. The problem to-day is to reach or find a conception of God adequate to the wider knowledge placed within the grasp of man in the present age. If we obtain such a conception, how shall we define the relation of God to the world, and to man?

Negatively, we may say that a solution which in any way makes the world to be the other of God, or which makes the world to be the evolution of the divine life, or makes God and the world to be aspects of one reality, will not suffice. For any solution that will satisfy the speculative and the practical interests of man, and meet his moral and religious needs, must recognize the freedom, the worth, and the independence of God. Any solution that falls short of that or confuses it must be rejected; and even if we can find no solution, we must hold fast to the belief that a solution is possible, though we may not be able to find it. Any solution that makes it impossible for man to draw near to God, or for God to draw near to man, refuses to recognize patent facts of experience, and must be rejected as inadequate. The idealistic solution may be accepted as an element in the case, but it must be supplemented. We may say that for God the world is, and add that God is not the world. We say that in God all things and persons live, and move, and have their being, and yet maintain the richness, the fulness of the divine life apart from the world. In fact, we must do so, if we are to do justice to all the elements involved in the case.

Thus we approach the question, not by the process which gives us such terms as being, substance, the unknowable, the unconditioned, the absolute, which are terms so familiar to readers of metaphysical discussions, and lead to no result. For to us in the very nature of the case all being is determinate being. It is characterized so and so, and every predicate is a definition of being. To speak of the absolute and unconditioned as synonymous with God, is simply to alter the conception of God. For God exists as a determinate Being, and His attributes are simply expressive of the determinate Being that He is. If we take the religious consciousness as our guide and as our means of interpretation, and take it in its highest reach as given in the New Testament, then we shall no longer speak of God as absolute, and so on, but we shall borrow the grand words, God is spirit, God is life, God is love. In other words we shall think of God as a determinate Being existing in relations, and these relations are abiding distinctions within the circle of the divine life. God is not an abstract unity, nor an absolute and inclusive self-consciousness, God is a living, concrete, complex Being, and in the Godhead there are relations and activities always in relations and always in action. The relations within the Godhead come to our help and rescue us from the paralysis of thought wrought by the abstractions of metaphysics, and we are not compelled to think in terms of an abstract order, nor driven to the necessity of deriving a manifold universe from a simplicity in which there are no relations.

In the Godhead, then, we already have a kind of

unity which does full justice to all the facts; it conserves the unity and makes room for all the interrelations in which the Godhead consists. The Godhead is not abstract identity; infinite differences are within God, and infinite manifoldness are embraced within one unity. The relations become more apprehensible to us when they are looked at from the ethical side. Then they become vivid, real, and intelligible. The ethical terms in which we set forth these determinations of the divine are Father, Son, and Spirit. Before fatherhood and sonship had any existence among men the fact in all its glory, in all its fulness, in all its meaning, was in eternal existence, and love has always been, for it has its native home in God. God is the eternal actuality of love.

Thus in the very conception of the Godhead as given us in the highest expression of the religious consciousness, we find a type of unity such as we have been in search of. Infinite differences held together in living relation, the self-surrender of one to another, measureless love abiding in all the movements within the divine life, and endless opportunities of self-communication. It may be possible to call this "experience," to use the words of Mr. Bradley, but it is no lonely experience of one in mere relation with a world, it is already and has always been a social experience. In the divine life as it is disclosed to us, or as it is set forth in the highest form of the religious consciousness, we have, not a simple type, but a manifold in unity, not an absolute, unlimited, but a determinate being existing in relations, and in reciprocal relation of intelligent, rational, and spiritual movement. Not in quantitative simplicity nor in metaphysical abstraction are we to think of the Godhead, but the highest conception we can form is that of love unbeginning, unending, love at its highest ideal. Such a conception helps us to make intelligible the train of thought contained in the passage quoted from the Master of Balliol on a former page. It makes it possible to think of "God as the principle of unity in all things, and yet as a living God in whose image man is made."

We may invert the sentence of Mr. Bradley and say that the absolute, if we may call God by that name, is personal, is moral, is beautiful, is good, is true. It would indeed be difficult to make these or any other propositions of the absolute as the absolute is construed by him. For in that experience which has no history, though it contains all histories in it, there can be no reciprocity, no communion, no love. Indeed, the descriptions of the absolute, contained in the book of Mr. Bradley, are mainly negative. Almost every proposition is negatived by some other proposition. But on the view stated above, it is possible to find our highest and our best realized without imperfection and without any drawback. In the divine life our ideals are already realized, whatever these ideals may be. Every power of man, every faculty, every ethical virtue, every spiritual quality, has its ideal; our imperfect knowledge has perfect knowledge as its ideal; reason as insight and as power leads on to perfect reason as its ideal; Fatherhood and sonship, imperfectly realized here, have always been in their perfect form. The infinite is the realized ideal of the finite forms which our ideals take. In the Christian conception of the Godhead, we have the joy of recognizing the realization of the ideals which haunt us with their shadowy forms as the perfection of what we know and experience here. Whatever personal life foreshadows, whatever social relations may indicate as to their perfect form, all beauty, all righteousness, all truth, have their home and their perfection in God.

But what of the cosmos, and what of man? In connection with the Christian conception of God how are we to think of a material world, and of the possibility of individual selves living together in one cosmos? How can we think the cosmos along with the Christian conception of God? Are we to think the cosmos as the other of God? Idealism says we must so think if we are to think at all. Such a necessity of thought lies on all who lead up to a universal self-consciousness, or to any representation which leaves God without an other. From that point of view an other is imperatively needed, the universal subject must have an object; without an object it could not realize itself. But the Christian conception postulates otherness in the very divine life, and in that determinate Being, who we reverently name God, there is the otherness which is the actualization of all possibilities of perfection. For the Christian conception the stress is laid on another side, and the solution of the problem takes another form. We do not try to find God from the world merely, or to argue from the articulated system to the thought which makes it a system, though that way is open to us too, nor do we merely look for a subject for which all objects are, for we have recognized in the manifoldness of the Divine, characteristics which lay no imperative of thought on us why we should demand a datum objective to God. God is; and ideals are realized in the Godhead, and would be so if there were no cosmos.

If so, why should there be a cosmos? Perhaps we cannot say. But this may be said, that we must find a reason in some other direction than that which makes a cosmos necessary for the realization of God. May we not find a sufficient reason for the existence of a world in the ethical character of God? Suppose we take the great word "God is love," and take it as the essential meaning of God, may we not find in it the explanation of the cosmos and of man? Love is transitive, passes out beyond itself, gives itself to its object, and strives to make that object blessed. Eternal love had its home in God, but love abounds more and more; may we not conceive this love as the creative impulse to the making of a cosmos? Love can be satisfied only by giving, may it not explain, or make conceivable to us, a noble necessity that led to the making of a world? To us there is a necessity which is the meaning of freedom, we speak it every time we use the word "ought." There is a service which is perfect freedom. We may say in a higher sphere that there was an ethical necessity for creation on the part of God to satisfy His need of loving and of communicating Himself to the beings who could receive Him. "Creation is due to the moral perfection of the Creator, who is so essentially love that He could not but create a world that He might create beatitude." (Fairbairn's "Christ in Modern Theology," p. 413.)

Looking at the cosmos as the outcome of the creative love of God, just as we looked at the Godhead as the synthesis of transcendence and immanence, how are we to think the relation of God to the world? Has there ever been a deeper, truer word spoken on this than the ancient word, " He spake and it was done, He commanded and it stood fast "? In our measure we also have an activity that makes things to be which once were not. All around us are the works of man. At his command cities, states, empires, poems, histories, philosophies, arise, and man's activity under conditions and under limitations may enable us to think of an activity through the exercise of which the cosmos may have arisen. In the service of love, the power, wisdom of God, set to work and the cosmos began to be made. The material world is for us a means of effecting our purpose and realizing our aim. But before we can use it we must understand its nature, its law, and its method of working. But its nature, law, and method of working is on the other side a revelation to us of a mode of thought higher than our thought, and of a purpose greater than we have yet learned to know. May not nature be simply a mode of communion between beings who can think, reason, and feel? The story of nature is a story that we are learning to read more clearly as the years pass on, and every new page which we slowly spell out is a fresh testimony to the depth and breadth of the thought that is embodied in the universe. I have said something of the wondrous story in former lectures, here I lay stress on the conception that what we call the material world is, after all, only a system of embodied thought, a language conveying a meaning which may be understood, and is so far understood. May not this material universe be simply a vehicle for the expression of a divine meaning, and may not it be there for a purpose beyond itself?

One thing we know, that the material universe is there for the expression of our meaning, and it will take up what we mean, preserve it for a millennium or two, and the record can be read by those who can wrest the secret from it. The bricks of Babylon, the pyramids and the papyri of Egypt, and remains of antiquity from many countries and ages, have lent themselves first to take the meanings read into them, have kept that meaning, and have yielded up that meaning to the judicious questioning of the men of this century. If matter can thus serve intellectual and moral ends impressed on them by finite intelligence, what is to hinder us from thinking that in its very nature and in all the history of its movement, it is intended to convey to finite thinkers a meaning put into it by a Thinker and a Maker who is the source of it and of them? Science is just the meaning which man has found in nature, and it presupposes that there is such a meaning. The world of nature is a determinate world, existing not in vague possibility, but constituted so and so, in definite relations, and in defined modes of action which we call laws; that is, it has a meaning.

Out of infinitely possible worlds there is this actual world in which we are, and the nature and history and evolution of it are all definite and in-telligible. What is that but to say that the Maker of the world proceeded in the making of the world as if He had the aim of enabling intelligent beings of a finite order so far to read and understand the method of His working. He bound Himself, having begun to make a world, to proceed on the lines which He first laid down, and to make each step presuppose what had gone before, and make the next step a consequence of all that had been accomplished. Permanence and progression are notes of the history of this universe, and the method of evolution has established this conclusion on a firmer basis than ever. From the point of view of Christian Theism nature is the middle term between God and man, an instrument in the hand of both for communion and knowledge. May we ask what is the relation of God to the material universe? Can we find an answer? We have already expressed our dissatisfaction with the idealistic answer, may we keep what they have gained, and still have an answer of our own? They have helped us to conceive the real as rational, and to think of the world as a rational world. Is not the rationality of the world conserved when we regard it as the embodiment of a divine thought, the fulfilment of a divine purpose, even though we refuse to regard it as the other of God, or as necessary to the realization of God? We may go still farther and say that God is immanent in the material universe so far as that universe is able to receive Him. He is present in the atoms of matter as the power which holds them in being, He is present in the chemical world as the power that shapes the laws of its working, present in the world of life as the sustaining power that upholds and guides them onward and upward. He is the God who ever strives to communicate Himself to His creation, and to make a creation which can receive His self-communication.

The making of a world which can receive the fulness of God is a long, slow, and painful process. The process is not yet complete. We may, however, see something of the divine patience and love that has toiled at the making of such a world. We see that it is a work of patient and infinite toil, and we set aside the notion of a fiat as altogether unsuitable to the making of an ethical world. Such a world cannot be so made, for it can be made only by its own coöperation. Even in the lowest reach of life living things move, act, grow, only by their own exertions, and every quality they possess must, if not acquired, at least be used by them. The upward striving of life is the commonplace of evolution. Though this may be stated in terms that are merely mechanical, and may be reduced to terms of an abstract struggle, yet it is true that life makes progress only by effort, and living beings can maintain themselves and make progress only by sustained and well-directed effort. They have to help to make themselves. If this be true of all life, even of life which is guided by pressure, and not by foreseen ends, how much more true is it of life self-conscious, rational, and ethical, life which is ruled by ideals presented as motives and acted on for the accomplishment of foreseen ends. Emphatically here is a life that cannot be made by mere power, or by pressure, or by instinct, or by the exercise of terror or fear. It must be won by rational motives and ideal ends set forth in such a way as win the desires and inform the motives, and to persuade the conscious being that this is the ideal which he is bound to realize.

If a world is to be made in this way,—and it is the only way in which such a world can be made,—clearly it is a process that must be slow. The education of the human race has been slow, painful, and laborious, but there has been an education of the human race. Progress has been made, ideals have been formed, and men have been trained to understand and love these ideals. It has been a real history to which all the races have made their contribution, and the end is not yet. It is a history from which we have yet much to learn, and when we read it, we ought to take heed lest we bring it down to the level of our own idealism, and reduce it to a formula of our own. Idealism has manifested that tendency many a time, notably in the case of Strauss and Green. But the trend of history is the exhibition of a larger idealism than ours, it is the idealism of God, worked out in the making of a world, to which He can communicate Himself. As the world of nature is larger than our science, and is the most constant and stringent critic of our science, so is history the greatest critic of our theories. On all sides nature and history remind us that we do not rule even this planet, and that there are larger meanings in the world than we have yet seen.

But we have read the story so far as to get a glimpse of the larger meaning. If we read it as the story of the making of a world which is to have a diviner issue than is yet seen, may we not hope that the apparent failures, the woes, the miseries, the mistakes, and the evil that stand written in lurid colours all over the pages of history may have a meaning? At all events, the making of an ethical and spiritual world, in which ethical ideals will be universally acted on, is a stupendous task. As I glance at the histories, philosophies, and religions of the world, I must say that I have not found much light cast on the awfulness of human history by any one of them, one only excepted. Not much help can be had from a philosophy which minimizes the sin and misery of the world, nor from one that exaggerates these until the other side is lost sight of altogether. But in one place and among a certain people there arose a way of thinking of man and his history and destiny which relieves the darkness of the outlook, and that without doing violence to the facts whether these are optimistic or pessimistic. That view teaches me to look at the world of nature and of man as the work of God, and it represents God as a living God, of Whom, to Whom, and through Whom are all things, and it represents God as not indifferent to the world of men. But the main thing at present for us is, that this God is represented as working and toiling through the ages in order to make man, and to raise man to that divine ideal formed for each man and for all men in the kingdom of God.

We are coming to understand that wondrous story, and the light which it casts on the character of God and the course of history. A living God striving to persuade an intelligent, rational creature to whom freedom has been given, of the kind of life he ought to live, and of the aims he ought to have, and to win him to surrender himself to the higher guidance, and to realize the chief end of his being. That is the vision disclosed to us in that literature. It is a story of the mistakes which man has made, a story of the way in which he has perpetually chosen lower ideals and has striven to realize them. A story on man's side of baffled aims and thwarted desires, of defeat and misery because he had made mistakes, and on the side of God, a constant, patient love, striving to raise man to the recognition of the higher ideals and of the life which a man ought to live. God bearing with men, striving, toiling, working, loving, shall I not say suffering? in order to make men who might receive Him, and striving to satisfy His desire to love and impart Himself to a people who could receive Him. So the course of history may be read, as the striving of God to educate men, and to raise them to the recognition of that ideal He has formed for man. May we not thus read the discipline of law, the connection between wrong-doing and misery, the pain of thwarted desire, and the pang of deferred hope? All these and the other phenomena of human life and history become luminous when read in the light of the purpose of God to make a kingdom of finite spirits to whom He could communicate Himself, and to whom He might give blessedness unspeakable.

This ethical world is making, it is not yet made. It is being made now by all the agencies at work in the world we know, and in the making of it a mother's love, a father's care, the answering love of children, the pity and piety that are in the world, loyalty to ideals, devotion to duty, the grandeur of science, the splendour of philosophy, the vision of beauty realized in art and poetry, the might of religion, and the magnificence of Christian effort are factors in the hand of God for the making of that kingdom of God which is to crown the cosmos and justify the toil of the ages. Unless we can have such a hope as the outcome of all the travail of the ages human effort would be paralyzed. Even with that hope clouds and darkness remain, and the difficulty of a speculative adjustment of all elements abide. That is simply to say that we are finite, and cannot look at all things from the centre.

At the same time, it is to be observed that the world to which the present state leads is a world of persons, intelligent, self-conscious, ethical, spiritual, and the unity of such a world presupposes a plurality of such persons, bound together by bonds which are not quantitative, but ethical and spiritual. The bond is constituted freely through self-surrender, and the recognition of the bond of service is the way of self-realization. In any ultimate unity there must be a recognition of the worth of each person, and each person must be conceived as ready to see that for the realization of his personality the whole is needed. " Be a person and recognize others as persons," it seems to me that no scheme of monism can give a real meaning to this ethical precept. We are in search of a unity, and the unity we require is of the most complex kind. For it must include in it God, man, and the world. No unity of the kind proposed by monism meets the necessity of the case. In fact, monism does injustice to the conception of God, for it makes Him to be nothing for Himself, it destroys the reality of finite life, and leaves it no room for self-development and self-surrender to a higher, and it makes the cosmos to be really acosmic. We must widen the meaning of unity, and follow on from the unity of abstract identity to the wider unity which meets us in scientific investigations, up to the unity of self-conscious life, up to the higher unity of many self-conscious lives in an organism which is spiritually held together, not by physical bonds in any way, but none the less held together in a real unity.

The history of the universe must be construed as a real history, and the events in it must have real validity.   How shall this be accomplished?   It seems to me that it has so far been accomplished by the recognition of the unity of many persons in a social unity.   There is, if anywhere, the type of unity of which we are in search.   A social unity constituted by God, to God, and for God, in which a finite world can come to its ideal in God, and be a world to which God can communicate Himself, and in which the world will gladly surrender itself to God, this is the unity we need, and we have it in the kingdom of God.   But can we have such a unity of God, man, and the world ?   Not if we make it a quantitative one. To such a unity Strauss's objection would be fatal. " If reality is ascribed to the idea of the divine and human natures, is this equivalent to the admission that this unity must have actually been once manifested, as it never had been, and never more will be, in one individual?   This is, indeed, not the mode in which the Idea realizes itself ; it is not wont to lavish all its fulness on one exemplar, and be niggardly to all others — to express itself fully in that one individual, and imperfectly in all the rest ; it rather loves to distribute its riches among a multiplicity of exemplars which reciprocally complete each other— in the alternate appearance and suppression of a series of individuals."   (Strauss's " Life of Jesus," George Eliot's " Translation," pp. 779–80.)

The objection reveals the character of the unity which is in his mind. It is simply a quantitative unity, and the riches of the idea are of a quantitative kind. Now there is a kind of wealth which is quantitative. If you have it, I have it not. If it is yours, it is not mine. This kind of wealth has nothing personal or distinctive about it, and it is equally at home in every pocket. There is another kind of wealth which is kept by giving it away. Intellectual wealth, moral wealth, spiritual wealth, is increased by imparting it to others. If the wealth of the idea could be lavished on one exemplar, that would be the shortest and surest way of enriching all the individuals in the world. It enriches me to think of Sir Isaac Newton, and the wealth of the "Principia" is mine when I can receive it. The thoughts of Plato and Aristotle, the poetry of Homer and Dante, the achievements of any man, the measure of perfection maintained by any man, — these are not an impoverishment of me, but a way of enriching me. The wealth of human thought, the greatness of human achievement, the grandeur of moral life realized in any life, are mine, if I can take them. And if I take them I do not make any man the poorer. Suppose all perfections realized in one man, suppose the wealth of the idea to be fully realized in one individual, then that would be a way of revealing to all men the greatness of humanity, and of inspiring them to follow and to imitate. The fulness of realized and manifested human life is the heritage of man, and it is of a kind to which the measure of quantity does not apply. Think of what Washington and Lincoln have been to this great land, and to the people in it.

Moral, intellectual, and spiritual wealth are qualitative, not quantitative. The criticism of Strauss becomes inept as soon as this is seen. The relations in the kingdom of God are qualitative, not quantitative. What is given and taken in that kingdom grows with the giving and taking, just as the intellectual, moral, and spiritual wealth of humanity increases from age to age; but the growth of such wealth here is but a shadow of the growth of that wealth in the perfected kingdom of God. God can give Himself in love, grace, and truth, and the giving does not lessen the fulness of God. Man can surrender himself to God, and in that surrender find perfect freedom and fulness of being. We have exemplars of that fact in human life here, and we can see it realized in part in the family, the state, and the church. Of course neither the person who surrenders himself nor the object to whom he surrenders himself is perfect, and the full ethical meaning of such a relationship is not disclosed here and now. But it is so far disclosed as to reveal to us the ideal of such a relationship under other conditions. Nay, there is one phase of such a possibility set forth even here, but it is one on which I do not dwell. Let me say that in the surrender of a man to Christ, and in the giving of Himself by Christ to man, we find a fact of religious experience in which an ideal is reached, and the man who surrenders himself to Christ finds himself in Christ.

Full scope for individual life, thought, and action, full realization of the individual in all his individuality, perfected character of each according to the ideal of the individual, and on the other side the wealth of the whole poured into each person, and returned by each person to the whole, and all in God, who gives himself in immeasurable fulness to His creation, such is the ideal of the kingdom of God. That unity is not the starting-point, it is the goal. It is not yet, but it will be. It will be the outcome of infinite striving, it will be the result of age-long divine endeavour, the fruit of eternal toil, work, and suffering, for it is the effort of God to make a world, which also makes itself, and must be persuaded to do so.

Much more might be said, had I more time. But I have already far exceeded my limits. In this last lecture I have been only able to give an outline of what I mean, but the outline I hope is intelligible, and, in the future, it may be worked out in more detail. But I am persuaded that it is on these lines that the philosophy and theology of the future may most hopefully proceed. Philosophically, we must retrace our steps somewhat, and try to make the metaphysic of Kant agree with his ethic, and give a rational meaning to the thing in itself, which is an irrational element in his system. Theologically, too, we have a great deal to do, and we must overhaul our abstract doctrines, rescue them from the dominion of abstractions, and make them to be a fuller representation of the reality of the concrete personal, religious life of the individual, and of individuals constituted into a society of redeemed men. The outlook is not dark, it is hopeful. Many are at work, many run to and fro, and knowledge is increased, and every increase of knowledge is available for the service of theology, and theology is giving itself to the mighty task of using it. For theology is in the central position, and has the widest command of the requisite resources; it can alone adequately deal with the postulates and the fulness of the religious life; and if unity is to be attained, it must be attained through theology.

INDEX

9 783337 080587